THE POWER BEYOND YOUR SUBCONSCIOUS MIND
A-MSY

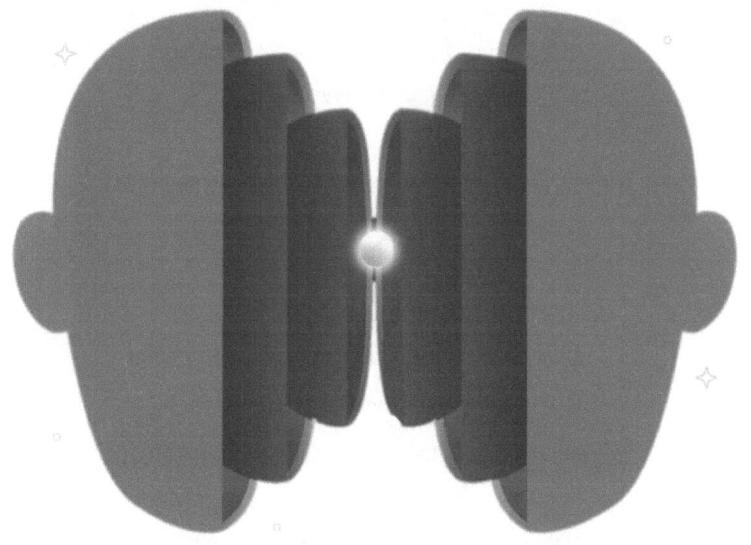

ACCESS YOUR INNATE POWER
TO SOLVE THE UNSOLVABLE

SIRSHREE
Author of the Bestseller *The Source*

The Power Beyond Your Subconscious Mind
A-MSY

Access Your Innate Power to Solve the Unsolvable
By **Sirshree** Tejparkhi

Copyright © Tejgyan Global Foundation
All Rights Reserved 2022

Tejgyan Global Foundation is a charitable organization
with its headquarters in Pune, India.

ISBN :   978-93-90607-43-3

Published by WOW Publishings Pvt. Ltd., India

First Edition published in December 2022

Printed and bound by Trinity Academy, Pune, INDIA

This book is the translation of the Hindi book titled
"AMSY - The Power Beyond Your Subconscious Mind" by Sirshree Tejparkhi.

Copyright and publishing rights are vested exclusively with WOW Publishings Pvt. Ltd. This book is sold subject to the condition that it shall not by way of trade or otherwise, be lent, resold, hired out, or otherwise circulated without the publisher's prior written consent in any form of binding or cover other than that in which it is published and without a similar condition including this condition being imposed on the subsequent purchaser and without limiting the rights under copyright reserved above, no part of this publication may be reproduced, stored in or introduced into a retrieval system, or transmitted, in any form, or by any means, electronic, mechanical, photocopying, recording or otherwise, without the prior written permission of both the copyright owner and the above-mentioned publisher of this book. Any person who does any unauthorized act in relation to this publication may be liable to criminal prosecution and civil claims for damages.

Although the author and publisher have made every effort to ensure accuracy of content in this book, they hereby disclaim any liability to any party for any loss, damage, or disruption caused by errors or omissions, resulting from negligence, accident, or any other cause. Readers are advised to take full responsibility to exercise discretion in understanding and applying the content of this book.

To
The Yogis
who realized the obscure powers of their astral bodies
through their yogic abilities and deep meditation,
and used these powers for the welfare of others.

Contents

Preface		7
Part 1	**The Glory of A-MSY**	**11**
1.	The Wondrous Design of the Human Mechanism	13
2.	The Influence of the A-MSY	18
3.	Some Truths about the A-MSY	23
4.	Why the A-MSY Holds A-Priority	27
5.	The Ultimate Remedy	31
6.	Six Steps To Tap Into the Power of the A-MSY	35
Part 2	**The Cure for the Incurable**	**43**
7.	The Root Cause of Diseases of the B-MSY	45
8.	Understanding the Nature of Diseases in the B-MSY and Their Cure	49
9.	Communicating With the A-MSY for Healing Illnesses	55
	Testimonial - 1	60
10.	Conversing With Other Peoples' A-MSYs	64
	Testimonial - 2	68
11.	Communicate To Be Healthy Forever	73
	Testimonial - 3	76
12.	Essential Qualities To Gain Effective Outcomes	79

Part 3	**Sending Vibrational Energy**	**83**
13.	Enliven Your Relationships	85
14.	Have Faith in the Boatman	90
	Testimonial - 4	94
15.	Children Are Little Bosses; Grownups Are Big Bosses	99
16.	Conquering Behavioral Patterns With Inner Strength	104
	Testimonial - 5	109
17.	A-MSY Communication for Emotional Maturity	113
18.	Sending Your Messenger by Saying What You Want	117
19.	Communicating With Our Ancestors' A-MSYs	121
	Testimonial - 6	126
20.	Conversing With Non-Living Objects	128
	Testimonial - 7	135
	Testimonial - 8	138
Part 4	**Using the Power of the A-MSY for Your Spiritual Awakening**	**143**
21.	Preparing for the Afterlife	145
22.	Training the Intuitive Mind	150
23.	Invoking the A-MSY of a Higher Consciousness	154
24.	Seeking Your A-MSY's Support for Spiritual Progress	158
	Testimonial - 9	162
25.	How To Attain Balance in All Spheres of Life	164
	Appendix 1	173
	Appendix 2	179

Preface
A Surprise Gift

"Where did you first find me? Why is the moon so far away? Where does one go after death?"

A child of 2-3 years finds everything new and wondrous around him. At this tender age, he can neither understand nor can we explain anything to him. Hence, his strange questions may even make us laugh.

You may cajole him by saying, "We got you as a blessing from God", "After death, one goes to God's heavenly abode", or "After death, one turns into a shining star and watches over us from up there."

Did you also have such questions as a child?

As we grow up, many mysteries of life begin to unfold. We begin to understand the world and nature of life after passing through school, university, and the various experiences that life brings. But then, while our childhood questions are put to rest, new questions arise within us. Our questions keep changing with time. We often find answers that do not fully satisfy us, and some unresolved questions keep haunting us.

"Where do we all come from? Where do we go after death? What is the difference between the mind and the brain? How does our body work all by itself? What is the secret of our enduring health? How did all beings come into existence? Who created them? Who runs the universe? Is there a power beyond the mind that enlivens and sustains us?"

Have you been preoccupied with such questions? Whatever your questions may be, they are often inscrutable. Our universe hides countless mysteries within its galaxies and stellar systems. But the most perplexing of them all is the inexplicable constitution of a human being!

Indeed, our bodies are the most precious and priceless gifts bestowed upon us. There are so many mysteries hidden within, many of which continue to remain unrevealed. The more we try to explore the secrets of the human body and mind, the more hitherto unknown wonders and abilities come to light.

Every mystery unfolds like a surprising gift before us when we need it the most! When we are overwhelmed by pleasant or unpleasant situations, the surprise gifts unfold within us in the form of hidden abilities that help us overcome those situations. We feel astonished at our own feat and wonder "How did this happen!" Let us understand this with an example.

Imagine you live amidst beautiful valleys in a mountainous region. You aspire to hoist the flag at the summit after scaling the highest mountain. You start training yourself in mountaineering. With a lot of practice, you are all set to climb the mountain range.

You pack your rucksack with essentials like clothes, a torch, a water bottle, a first-aid kit, etc. Some friends, relatives, and others also accompany you. Enthusiastically, you embark on your journey.

Preface

You enjoy the scenic beauty on the way, trekking through the weathered rocks. As you climb higher, the journey becomes fascinating, although risky. Various kinds of thoughts trouble you. "Will I be able to survive at the peak?", "Will I reach my goal and hoist the flag?", "What will it be like when I succeed?", or "What if my wish to succeed remains unfulfilled?" You keep going with these mixed feelings.

Midway on the track, there comes a point where you are neither able to move forward nor retreat. You are stranded. You are confused and do not know what to do! After pondering for a while, you begin to grope around in your bag as if searching for something.

And there you find a little book titled "Surprise Gift" in one of the pockets. The title makes you curious. As you slowly read through the chapters, you find the exact guidance you need to tackle various possible situations on this journey and how to overcome them. You happily follow the guidance and successfully move forward from that impasse.

The surprise gift was already there with you all along, but you were unaware of it. You came to know about it only in the face of the calamity. Similarly, each of us has a surprise gift within us.

What is this surprise gift?

When you face problems in the journey of life, you may get stranded, neither able to move forward nor turn back. It is then time to unwrap the surprise gift. This surprise gift is the supreme power beyond your subconscious mind! It is a latent power.

Being unaware of this power, we keep struggling with problems that can be easily resolved. We keep struggling, relying on our senses, minds, and physical abilities. Sometimes we succeed, and sometimes we don't.

If you, too, are caught up in a disease, trouble, or challenge that seems incurable or unsurmountable, you must awaken your latent power and learn the art of using it.

If you can use this power in every situation, you will find it easy to resolve every problem – be it strained relationships, workplace challenges, financial issues, business challenges, difficulty in learning necessary skills, or an illness.

You need to properly understand this mysterious and latent surprise gift you have within you, the power of which goes beyond your subconscious mind. It will work like a magic wand for you! It will make the journey of your life easy and empower you to help others in their times of need.

This book unveils this art and the mysteries of the human body one by one. While understanding them, you can unwrap your surprise gift and enjoy your life to the fullest. So, let's begin…

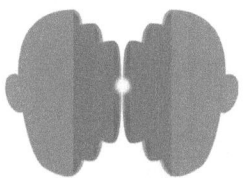

PART 1
The Glory of A-MSY

1

The Wondrous Design of the Human Mechanism

Whatever has been created in the world is almost similar in constitution. Be it the flora, the fauna, or the microorganisms, everything is made up of the five elements of earth, water, fire, air, and ether. These five elements are present in varying proportions in every micro or macro organism.

The human body is also made up of these five elements. Everyone looks different externally, their lifestyles are different, and they think differently; but fundamentally, we all are constitutionally similar.

Let us understand the mechanism of the human body with the analogy of a mobile phone. Several brands of mobile phones are available in the market. But each needs three essential parts to function: the screen, the battery, and the SIM card. Similarly, the human body consists of three basic parts—the physical body, the subtle body, and pure consciousness.

Part 1 – The physical body

The mobile phone's screen and metallic body are visible. All the downloaded apps can be seen on the screen.

Similarly, our physical body is visible to everyone around us. We can call it the B-priority Body-Mind or gross body. It is the tangible body-mind mechanism, perceptible to the human senses. The human body is incomplete without the mind (thoughts and feelings), and hence, it is called the Body-Mind Mechanism.

The Body-Mind Mechanism is called *Mano Sharir Yantra* (*MSY*) in Hindi. We will refer to the physical body or the Body-Mind Mechanism as B-MSY in this book.

Usually, everyone assumes themselves to be their B-MSY because they see all their tasks being carried out by their physical body. They perceive the color, form, mechanism, strength, weaknesses, nature, and skills of their B-MSY. Hence, even if not completely, they at least know partly about their B-MSY.

Part 2 – The A-MSY

The second important part of the mobile is its battery. It is not externally visible, but the mobile can be used only when charged.

Our inner body is like the battery. It is imperceptible to the human senses. But the physical body functions only because of this inner body. The inner body can also be called the A-Priority Body-Mind, subtle body, or astral body. We will call it the A-MSY in this book.

Just as a mobile is dead without its battery, so is the B-MSY dead without the A-MSY. But we are unaware of the existence and mechanism of the A-MSY.

Part 3 – Pure Consciousness

The third most important part of the mobile phone is its SIM card due to which it is connected to the service network. Although its microwave radiation is invisible, it is only the connection with the service network that enables us to connect with everyone else.

Just like the SIM card, our inner core is pure consciousness. It is the substratum of life due to which we are connected to nature. The A-MSY and B-MSY cannot survive without pure consciousness. Pure consciousness is the divine experience, the sense of our beingness, or life force.

Let us now understand these aspects of the human body in detail.

The physical body or B-MSY

As discussed earlier, the B-MSY is composed of the five fundamental elements – earth, water, fire, air, and ether (space); space being the subtlest and earth the grossest of these elements.

The expression of these five elements in various combinations gives rise to physiological components called *Doshas*: *Vata*, *Pitta*, and *Kapha*. The combination of space and air forms Vata. Water and fire constitute Pitta. Water and earth combine to create Kapha. The health of the human Body-Mind rests on the delicate balance of these doshas. An imbalance in the relative proportions of the doshas impacts our mental and physical well-being.

The B-MSY also includes the *pranic* layer (the vital energy sheath) comprising the *chakras* (energy vortices) and meridians (energy channels). The chakras are whirling vortices of energy that take in universal energy and distribute it to the rest of the *pranic* layer through the meridians.

Our physical body and its physiological processes are the gross manifestation of energy. Several processes such as respiration, blood circulation, digestion, etc. occur within the body to make the B-MSY function.

As the B-MSY is visible to us, we become engrossed in maintaining its health and beauty. We put in our best efforts to satiate its incessant sensory cravings. The B-MSY also experiences certain illnesses, pains, and problems but we can safeguard it from them by taking good care of it.

The subtle body or A-MSY

The core of a tree laden with beautiful flowers and lush fruits is its roots. The flowers and fruits come into existence only when properly nourished by the roots. The roots are the subtle part of the tree that is invisible to us, whereas flowers, fruits, and leaves are the gross part that is visible.

Similarly, in the physical realm, the A-MSY is invisible to our gross senses of sight, hearing, and touch. Yet, it expresses itself through the B-MSY. It is like a breeze that is invisible and yet is expressed through the movement of leaves. The A-MSY is instrumental in driving human life, making decisions, expressing feelings, and shaping thoughts. The A-MSY is flexible and impressionable. This means it is subject to being molded by the impressions it receives from the B-MSY. Positive impressions mold the A-MSY positively, while negative inputs can mold it in harmful ways.

The human mind and body are an expression of pure consciousness. As energy becomes denser, it takes the form of thoughts, feelings, emotions, and intellectual faculties. This constitutes the A-MSY.

Our conscious and subconscious minds are part of the A-MSY. Our thoughts, understanding, feelings, and tendencies affect the A-MSY first. Hence, it is easiest to correct them at the level of the A-MSY because the power of the A-MSY transcends both the conscious and subconscious minds.

Pure Consciousness

Pure consciousness, also known as the Source, is neither the gross nor the subtle part of the body. Rather, it can only be known through experience. It is beyond the inner and outer world.

Without pure consciousness, the body is dead. Pure consciousness does not interfere with any of the body's functions, yet the body cannot function without it. It is also known as the "bliss sheath."

The source of thoughts, feelings, and physical actions exists beyond the mental and physical realm. The Source pervades all manifestation.

Awareness is the essence of the Source. Pure awareness, or pure wakefulness, brings about the manifestation of forms and phenomena. Our mind, comprising of thoughts and feelings, is the expression of pure awareness. Our body is a denser and perceptible expression of the Source, a grosser expression of the subtle mind.

Let us understand this with the example of an almond. The almond fruit has three layers to it – the outer sheath known as the husk, the seed that houses the nut, and the delicious nut itself. These layers are revealed when you break the fruit open. You can get the almond nut only after the first two sheaths are removed. In this example, the husk is the B-MSY, the seed within is the A-MSY, and the almond nut we taste is pure consciousness.

When we see the fruit from outside, the seed and the nut, though present, are not visible. Similarly, our B-MSY is visible externally, while the A-MSY and pure consciousness cannot be seen.

We can experience pure consciousness through meditation. When we delve deep into meditation, we can detach from both the A-MSY and the B-MSY, and dwell in pure consciousness. Knowing pure consciousness through our own experience is the ultimate goal of human life.[1]

---

[1] In addition to the A-MSY and the B-MSY, a third body also exists which is called the Causal Body. It holds the impressions of all the karmas and memories of our Body-Mind, which later become the cause for an afterlife. This is beyond the scope of this book and hence is not discussed.

2

The Influence of the A-MSY

At what stage of life are you today – adolescence, adulthood, or old age? Have you been at the same stage since birth?

You may wonder, "What an absurd question this is! How can one remain the same throughout their life? Everyone is born an infant and their state changes with the passage of time."

Yes. The human body changes with time as we age. Everyone passes through six different stages of life – infancy, teenage, youth, adulthood, old age, and the death of the gross body or B-MSY. The first stage after birth is infancy, then we grow into teenage, and further grow into youth. We then mature into the fourth stage of adulthood and grow further into old age. At the sixth stage, the gross body dies. But life does not end when the B-MSY perishes because the further journey of the subtle body, the A-MSY, begins there.

Besides these six stages of growth, there is also a seventh stage in which one experiences one's true Self. One recognizes the Self beyond the body and mind through direct experience. This is the state of Self-realization that can emerge during any of the six stages of life.

While passing through the initial five stages, we do not grieve for the loss of life, "Oh! I lost my childhood in becoming a youth. Alas! I've lost my youth by becoming an adult. I've lost the prime of my life by becoming old." This is because we know that it is yet another stage of life. And most importantly, we can clearly perceive each of these stages with our physical senses. These stages are tangible. However, sorrow creeps in when we see our close ones die and their gross body transforms into the subtle body in the sixth stage. This is only because the subtle body is intangible and imperceptible to the human senses.

The death of the physical body (B-MSY) is just a process of shifting to the frequency of the subtle body (A-MSY) which is not perceptible to human senses. At this stage, the outer body perishes, but the inner body and pure consciousness are still alive in a different realm, vibrating at a higher frequency. We will explore this in detail in the last part of this book. Now, we will understand how the subtle body affects our gross body and our life on earth.

While the subtle body is connected to the gross body, they keep influencing each other. Whatever feelings, sensations, or tendencies arise in the subtle body get reflected as symptoms in the gross body. Thus, the activities of the gross and subtle bodies keep affecting one another.

Let us understand this with the analogy of a motorbike-car.

Consider you are driving a motorbike having a handle like the steering wheel of a car. Suppose someone attaches the body of a car around the motorbike. How will it appear externally? It will appear as if you are driving a car, whereas you are really riding a motorbike. You see cars moving around you, but they are also motorbikes.

You drive very cautiously to avoid any jerk to the car's body. You are aware that the slightest jerk to the car's body may make you lose the balance of the motorbike. At the same time, even the faintest jitter in the motorbike's engine can shake the car.

For driving the car, you will need to fill fuel in the motorbike's tank because the car's engine is also embedded in the motorbike. If the motorbike is in perfect running condition, the car will support you throughout the journey. Similarly, if the car's body is in good condition, you can travel and reach your destination unhindered.

The same mechanism is present in the human Body-Mind. Here, the car represents the gross body or the B-MSY, and the motorbike represents the subtle body or the A-MSY. The one driving both the A-MSY and the B-MSY represents pure consciousness. Just as the car appears to be moving on the outside, the gross body also seems to move and perform all the tasks on the outside. But in reality, the A-MSY drives the B-MSY. Whenever there are glitches in the B-MSY, it impacts the A-MSY first. Later, the impact aggravates, and the symptoms appear on the B-MSY.

The inputs received through the senses of the B-MSY, the upbringing from our childhood, and daily situations keep influencing the A-MSY. If the input is negative, it gradually reflects on the gross body as diseases, anxiety, or failure. And if the input is positive, it manifests as success, good health, happiness, and prosperity.

The A-MSY is invisible. Hence, we mistake the B-MSY to be everything and spend our entire life adorning it and satiating its desires. We do not even mind blindly following the masses for this. The gross body is least aware of the inputs it is constantly feeding into the subtle body. Hence, by repeatedly harboring negative thoughts, it attracts the same incidents in life. Instead, if we dwell in love, bliss, and positivity, our subtle body will always remain pure and easily attract a successful, prosperous, and blissful life.

Nature has blessed the A-MSY with countless unknown powers that can bring about a revolution in the world. Just like the head of the state or a country is bestowed with enormous powers to work for the welfare of all, nature has empowered the A-MSY in ways that it can become instrumental for the well-being of the entire world, besides ourselves.

Now, it all depends on the inputs we choose to feed into the A-MSY so that our earthly life attains the supreme state.

3

Some Truths about the A-MSY

New discoveries or inventions are not accepted instantly. People find it difficult to accept them in the beginning. But when these topics are repeatedly discussed and evidence is brought to the forefront, people gradually develop faith in them.

Today, many holistic healers, psychologists, and spiritual masters emphasize that a subtle body exists in every human being. The mechanism of the subtle body is exactly like that of the gross body and it has innumerable qualities.

Nowadays, many people have started believing this. However, some people are still stuck in the wrong beliefs or ignorance regarding the existence of the subtle body. Let us unravel these myths and misunderstandings and understand more about the A-MSY.

1. Myths about the soul

As human life makes progress, our vocabulary keeps changing. We interpret some old words differently, and at times, we even replace them with new words. One such word is "soul". In ancient times, the subtle body was denoted by the word "soul". But with the passage of time, its meaning has changed. In many traditions, it has been given a negative connotation and linked to the idea of ghosts and discarnate entities.

Many movies depict people turning into ghosts after death, scaring people and seeking revenge on their wrongdoers. Such movies delude people and instill numerous myths regarding death.

Although such negatively portrayed ghosts are never a part of life on earth, movie makers paint a dreadful portrayal to cause a nerve-shattering effect on the audience. People borrow these negative beliefs and restrain themselves from delving into this subject because it makes them uncomfortable. Thus, they avoid gaining clarity on this subject.

Are you also among them? Are you afraid of subtle bodies or discarnate entities as depicted in movies or TV serials? If so, you need to first gather some knowledge on this subject. Subtle bodies never wish to scare us as they attain clarity of life and its purpose when they shift into the astral plane. Instead, they wish to help us with their positive intentions. You can immensely benefit by understanding your subtle body.

2. The existence of the subtle body after death

Today, almost all religious faiths have accepted the existence of life after death. Hence, after the death of the physical body, certain prayers are offered and rituals are performed for the peaceful onward journey of the soul. It is also emphasized that we should perform only positive karma during life on earth so that the A-MSY can journey peacefully after death. If not all, some people have accepted the existence of the subtle body.

People often assume that the soul or the subtle body comes into existence only after death, not before that. And if it does not exist while one is alive, how can one speak about its powers? But the truth is that the subtle body exists alongside the gross body while we live on earth. We can benefit from the enormous powers of the A-MSY and bring happiness, prosperity, health, success, and contentment in our life. This book explains how to invoke and harness these powers.

3. Is it true that mediums can converse with subtle bodies in the astral plane?

This is true as well as false. How can it be so? Actually, many things happen on earth which may be true for some and false for others. People believe or reject them based on their own experiences. Mediumship is one such phenomenon.

When our outer, physical body dies, our inner body vibrates at a different frequency. Some people with extra-sensory perception can serve as mediums to interact with these subtle bodies. They have pronounced psychic powers which most people do not. They serve as channels for two-way communication between the subtle world and our physical world. Mediumship is more popular and openly received in Western societies than in Eastern societies because of the predominant social taboo and intrinsic fears about occult practices prevalent among Eastern cultures.

Although these extra-sensory abilities can be used for the well-being of people, many people misuse them to earn money. There are conmen, who claim to be able to convey messages to our loved ones in the subtle world without really doing so. If you know of an authentic medium, you can take their help.

4. Astral travel

Astral travel is the experience of going beyond the physical body. Very often, our subtle body travels to different places leaving our gross body behind when it is in a deep-sleep state.

Many people have lucid experiences of having been to distant places even before they physically visited them. They feel they have already been to a particular place, though they cannot reason how and when they would have visited it. This is because their subtle body has already visited those places when their gross body was asleep. Hence, they are unable to remember it. This experience is also called *Déjà vu*, which means *already seen*.

The subtle body is connected to the gross body with an invisible, delicate silver cord, also known as a spiritual cord. While asleep or in deep meditation, our subtle body journeys out. At such times, if our physical body happens to move or is interrupted, the subtle body immediately returns to the gross body within a fraction of a second.

In case, you have unknowingly engaged in astral travel so far, with this understanding, you can consciously harness its benefit to gain more profound knowledge and solve your life problems. We will understand this in detail in a later part of this book.

While we are gradually delving deeper into this subject, it is more important to develop faith in the powers of the A-MSY and use them to bring a positive transformation in our life instead of examining the validity of the A-MSY itself.

4

Why the A-MSY Holds A-Priority

A few decades ago, people were unaware of the subconscious mind and its powers. But today, it has become one of the most discussed topics. Even science has delved deep into research and experimentation regarding the subconscious mind.

People have developed faith in it and have also accepted its powers. But the powerful subconscious mind is just a servant to its master, the A-MSY. This may be hard to believe, but it is a fact. The A-MSY is the power beyond the subconscious mind that can bring about miraculous results in our life.

Science has not yet proven the existence of the A-MSY. However, ancient ascetics have elaborated the journey of the subtle body, also known as astral travel.

Meditation practitioners who dive deep into it experience the powers of the subconscious mind at one time or another and use them for their growth, knowingly or unknowingly.

Let us understand the difference between the A-MSY and the subconscious mind with the help of an example. Suppose you have taken a dealership of small electrical appliances. You have established your credibility in the market. Retailers blindly trust your goods. But on one occasion, you receive a flurry of complaints on the mixer-grinders you dispatched. Initially, you are unable to figure out the reason but upon investigation, you find that the entire lot is defective.

Now, you contact the manager of the manufacturing company but to no avail. Then you remember that you had once met the owner of that company at an event and you have his contact details. You contact the owner and speak to him. The owner immediately contacts the manager and asks him to sanction the order to replace the faulty lot with a fresh one.

While you were unable to solve your problem despite repeated communication with the manager, your problem was instantly resolved by contacting the owner just once. That is the difference between the decisions of a manager and an owner! Although the owner consulted his manager before making the decision and also implemented it by taking the manager's help, only he could make such a decision. The manager might have exercised his authority in making other decisions, but he couldn't have made such a big decision without the owner's approval.

When we directly contact the owner, his subordinate can't deny his instructions because the subordinate reports to the owner and has to follow everything he is asked to do.

Similarly, the A-MSY is the master, and the subconscious mind is its subordinate. The subconscious mind has enormous powers, but it uses them only when it is asked to do so. Therefore, when we communicate with the A-MSY and seek its help, it easily fulfills our requirements by coordinating with the subconscious mind. The

A-MSY and subconscious mind can seek each other's help and easily overcome all the problems in our life.

Some people know about the conscious and subconscious mind. They are aware that for accomplishing any work, our conscious mind contributes 10% and the subconscious mind contributes 90%. If we want to get some work done by our subconscious mind, we must repeatedly affirm it. We can take the help of our subconscious mind to change our habits and beliefs by way of self-suggestions. If the subconscious mind's programming is changed, the conscious mind can't behave differently. However, not many people are aware that we can take the help of the powers of the A-MSY to change our subconscious mind's programming easily and effectively.

Now, you know that the subconscious mind is just an effective subordinate and the A-MSY is its master. So, why not contact the master directly so that all your tasks can be easily and successfully accomplished?

Yet, one may question, "If things can be done by programming the subconscious mind, why should we choose the A-MSY? After all, they are the same!"

No! There is a difference between the two. Generally, people believe that the subconscious mind controls the human body. Hence, its programming is important. Today, many techniques for programming the subconscious mind are popular worldwide. Science has conducted immense research about its powers and people have also benefited from them. However, the A-MSY is beyond the subconscious mind. The subconscious mind is merely a part of the A-MSY. You can communicate with the A-MSY to change the subconscious mind's programming easily. You can do so by harnessing the powers of both the A-MSY and the subconscious mind. This, in turn, reinforces the spirit of work multifold.

Although, science has not conducted any research on the A-MSY, it doesn't underestimate its glory. There was a time when no scientific research was conducted on the subconscious mind and its powers. Yet, our sages and saints, who were spiritual scientists, had already spoken of the powers of the subconscious mind with their experiences centuries ago. It took centuries after that for science to prove its existence and bring it to the forefront as a scientific theory. History bears witness to the fact that every revelation from the experience of the saints has always passed the test of time.

Years ago, Maharshi Patanjali had explained the glory of the "Eight limbs of Yoga" for attaining holistic health, but very few practiced it then. When science approved of it after much debate and experimentation, everyone started believing in it. Today, it is practiced worldwide.

Similarly, there will be scientific research conducted on the A-MSY, too, in the coming years. But we don't need to wait until then! We must connect with the A-MSY, harness its benefits, and gain first-hand experience.

5

The Ultimate Remedy

Whenever you have a question about anything, whom do you ask first? Perhaps, a well-wisher, a colleague, or an experienced person. And if you don't find their answers effective or if none of your acquaintances can give you satisfying answers, then what do you do?

You may say, "There is no need to ask anyone. With today's advanced technology, I can search for the answers on the internet."

But do you know that apart from these external websites, there exists a website *within* you that can answer all your questions satisfactorily? You don't need to use the internet for that. You can get such accurate guidance on every aspect of your life through this inner website that you may wonder, "From where does such vast knowledge flow into me?!"

This is the truth. The A-MSY is our personal website with exhaustive knowledge that is far greater than any web-based search engine. It is our constant companion. Hence, it has comprehensive information about every aspect of our life. But, until we connect with it, it does not interfere in our matters.

Once we start communicating with the A-MSY, we can easily answer all the questions of our life with its help. It can solve the biggest problems of our life and help us progress in every aspect. With its help, we can bring happiness, prosperity, peace, and harmony to all our relationships.

Let us understand how we can seek the support of the A-MSY in all facets of our life.

1. The physical facet

People usually suffer from some or the other health issue at the physical level. Some suffer from chronic illnesses, body aches, obesity, or weakness, while others suffer from incurable diseases like heart problems, cancer, or stroke. Some suffer from seasonal illnesses like sinusitis, asthma, allergies, skin diseases, etc. All these diseases can be cured with the help of the A-MSY.

We know that our body naturally heals any injury it may sustain. Nature has bestowed this incredible healing intelligence upon all beings, including animals, birds, and humans. When a virus infects our body, the required power of immunity to combat it is automatically triggered within the body. The power of immunity of the A-MSY is a thousand times higher than that of the gross body, the B-MSY! Hence, we can communicate with the A-MSY, seek its help, and cure the gross body at the earliest.

2. The mental facet

Sometimes some sorrowful events or hurtful feelings leave deep scars on our mind. With time, those memories fade away, but their impressions are permanently etched in the subconscious mind. Sometimes, these scarred memories influence our feelings to such an extent that we become unknowingly vulnerable at the mental level. Negative feelings of fear and inferiority overpower us, and we lose self-confidence.

Suppose you are suffering from certain sorrowful or hurtful memories from past incidents and they are posing hurdles in different areas of your life. In that case, you can interact with your A-MSY and bring a positive transformation to every facet of your life.

By communicating with your A-MSY, you can create the life you wish to live; you can get rid of negative impressions that don't serve your purpose; you can augment the qualities you want to express in your life. You can shape the rest of your future with the help of your A-MSY.

3. The social facet

Everyone aspires to have loving relationships with everyone. They wish for all kinds of comforts for their family members to ensure harmony in their relationships. They wish for lasting peace and happiness in their lives. This can become possible by seeking help from their A-MSY and that of the people around them.

4. The financial facet

You can pray to your A-MSY for abundance. You can become financially independent with its help. If you wish to help others financially, your A-MSY can support you. Thus, your A-MSY can help you to progress at the financial level in all possible ways.

5. The spiritual facet

With regular practice of meditation and prayer, you can bring about a new beginning in your life. If you want to realize your true Self, if you want to always retain a higher level of awareness, if you wish to seek the real purpose of your life, then your A-MSY can fully support you in this endeavor.

You can consider your A-MSY to be a close, trustworthy friend. Befriend it as your eternal companion. Share all your secrets with it. It is a friend who always accompanies you. It is such a pleasant feeling to have someone so caring, so loving, who is always there for us! You can share everything with this friend, who is available to you 24/7, and seek its help for all your problems. Have faith that as a true friend, your A-MSY listens to you and guides you accordingly.

6

Six Steps To Tap Into the Power of the A-MSY

Imagine that your close friend is always with you whenever you are in distress or grief. It makes you feel reassured and boosts your strength to endure the suffering. If the company of an external friend can ease your troubles so much, how relieving would it be to have a companion like your subtle body who is ever present, capable, and ready to help you?

But you may ask, "When I can neither hear nor see my A-MSY, how can I communicate with it? How can I convey my message to it?"

You may have heard some of these sayings – "Ask and you shall receive." "Knock on the door and it will be opened!" "You won't get it till you ask for it!"

Even God is invisible, yet we pray to Him! God also waits for us to sow the seeds in the form of prayers before answering them. He then works over them and sends them to us multifold. God bestows us with everything. But when we wish to attain something special in life, we need to align with Him and tell Him elaborately what we want. Only then are our desires fulfilled.

Parents always give their children everything even before they ask for it. But when the children want something special or something they like, they have to ask their parents for it. Then the parents fulfill their wish. Until we express our needs and wants clearly in words, the other person is unaware and cannot fulfill them. Clear communication between both people is necessary.

The same is the case with the A-MSY! Although it always accompanies us and knows everything about us, it does not work on what we want unless we ask for help. When we wish to interact with it, it will listen to us attentively and work accordingly.

Let us understand how to communicate with the A-MSY and get our work done in six steps with the help of an analogy.

Imagine there is a wedding in your family. You need to plan and execute everything, right from the start to the end of the ceremony with the help of your close relatives. How would you interact with them? You need to do the same with your A-MSY.

Step 1: Invite and welcome

First, you will invite all your close relatives to join you two to three days before the ceremony. They will accept your invitation and join you. As they arrive, you will welcome them heartily.

Similarly, you need to invite your special friend, your A-MSY, with the utmost love and respect, into your field of awareness. Try saying, "My dear divine A-MSY, I invite you into my field of awareness."

The A-MSY is always present within you but is invisible. Hence, you won't be able to perceive it physically, but have faith that it can hear you. Know and feel that your A-MSY is present and listening to you. Start communicating with it.

Step 2: Convey what you want

During the wedding, you openly discuss and seek help from those you trust the most. You tell them, "Thank you so much for joining us early. I was so stressed! It would have been difficult for me to manage everything all alone. But now, together, we can manage everything smoothly. I am feeling relaxed and charged in your presence." By interacting with them in this manner, knowing their nature and capabilities, you delegate various responsibilities to them.

Similarly, share openly with your A-MSY what you expect from it. Elaborately explain to it the areas where you need its assistance. For example, you may need its help to cure certain health issues, resolve conflicts within relationships, remove hurdles in your work, or seek clarity to fulfill some desires. You may be seeking support for your development and progress, guidance in some areas of life, or for performing prayers and practicing meditations to progress on your spiritual path. Clearly say what you want.

If you wish for better results from your A-MSY, communicate with it according to your nature. Broadly, people have three types of dispositions:

a. **Visual**

   Some people find it easier to imagine and visualize. They can easily relate to something seen visually and remember it. If you belong to this nature, while speaking to your A-MSY in words, also visualize that after listening to you, your A-MSY has started working on it. Whatever you wished for is being worked upon or has been fulfilled.

b. **Auditory**

   Some people like to listen to positive things. They can easily learn and understand whatever is being said and even reiterate it word for word. This is so because their hearing is more effective and efficient.

If this is your disposition, while speaking to your A-MSY, you can repeat many positive affirmations. For example, "Day by day, my health is getting better and better." "I am experiencing abundant love, joy, and peace in my life." Similarly, reiterate whatever you wish by using such positive words.

c. Kinesthetic

These people perceive everything through touch and feeling, and remember it. They use their emotions effectively and engage in creative endeavors. They pay more attention to their feelings. If you are kinesthetic, then connect to your A-MSY with feelings. If possible, touch and caress your body with love. Thank it, bless it. Heartily seek forgiveness for your carelessness.

Based on the above information, identify your natural disposition and communicate with your A-MSY accordingly.

Step 3: Seek forgiveness

During the wedding preparations, sometimes your relatives make a few decisions which you may not like or which hinder your work. You react rudely to them. But you also seek their forgiveness to keep them happy. You request them to ignore what you said to them.

Likewise, you have to seek forgiveness from your A-MSY for two things:

- All this while, you have neither communicated to your A-MSY nor thanked it for its unwavering care and support. Hence, seek its forgiveness by saying, "Dear A-MSY, I've never thanked you for your unwavering support. Please forgive me for that."

- You now intend to resolve issues, with the support of your A-MSY, that arose due to your mistakes. Seek forgiveness for that. You can say, "Dear A-MSY, you had to suffer due to my mistakes. Please forgive me for that."

Step 4: Assert and ask to begin the work

After seeking forgiveness from your relatives, you assure them of your trust in them by saying, "I have complete faith in you. I understand perfectly that whatever you have done is out of love. However, due to stress and inadequate information, I was upset with you. Please forgive me, let go of your resentment, and continue your good work." When you heartily seek forgiveness from your displeased relatives, they support you more.

Similarly, revive the capabilities of the A-MSY by asserting its powers. Say, "You have immense powers. You have the power to heal everything. Please support me in solving this problem with your powers."

Assertion has a power that catalyzes the healing process multifold. For example, when you motivate your friend by affirming, "You can surely accomplish this task easily," his enthusiasm multiplies and unleashes his hidden capabilities! In the same way, you must remind your A-MSY of its divine powers by asserting with complete faith, "You have the power to heal yourself and the B-MSY. You can cure any ailment."

Step 5: Chant and send the A-MSY out of your field of awareness

After making all the arrangements for the wedding, you enjoy the wedding ceremony with all your relatives with full enthusiasm. After completing all the rituals, you bid farewell to all your relatives.

Similarly, spend some time with your A-MSY in silence, chanting the words love, joy, and peace to invoke their feeling within yourself. Use this opportunity to be in the present. You can decide the duration of your chanting based on the time you have.

Love, joy, and peace are our innate qualities. Here, love represents unconditional, boundless love, which is beyond attachment. It is the power that creates and sustains the manifested universe. Unconditional joy transcends the polarities of happiness and sorrow. It is joy that is experienced without any prerequisites. Peace refers to the pure stillness, the nature of existence at the core of one's being. It exists beyond the duality of noise and silence.

These qualities are always readily available. We unconsciously block them from expressing themselves in our lives due to our limiting beliefs. By chanting the words love, joy, and peace we instruct the A-MSY to consciously allow love, joy, and peace to work through the A-MSY and facilitate the fruition of our prayer.

To the extent that you deeply feel love, joy, and peace, they begin to manifest in your field of awareness. Allow sufficient time for this invocation. Continue to chant for at least two to three minutes. Let only the three words remain in your space as you chant: love, joy, peace.

Now, assure your A-MSY again that you trust it fully. It can do everything. Then request it to leave your field of awareness and continue working even after that.

The A-MSY is the manifestation of divine intelligence. You can communicate with it and entrust tasks to it, just as you would with your best friend. Ask the A-MSY to continue working on whatever you have entrusted it even after you are done with your communication so it functions even when you are unaware of the process.

Step 6: Gratitude

After the wedding ceremony, you express gratitude to all your guests and relatives. You bid them farewell with gifts and ask them to remain connected thereafter.

Similarly, express gratitude to your A-MSY and B-MSY. The feeling of gratitude is magical! It does not allow negative energies to overpower you. This automatically dissolves most problems.

Thank your A-MSY for always supporting and helping you despite your non-awareness and carelessness.

When you thank your family and relatives for supporting you in any function or ceremony and appreciate them for their help, your joy multiplies. Similarly, when you trust your A-MSY completely like a friend and seek its guidance or opinions, it will be ready to support you every moment.

Keeping in mind the six steps of the wedding analogy, keep communicating with your A-MSY. Let's understand more about it in the next part of the book.

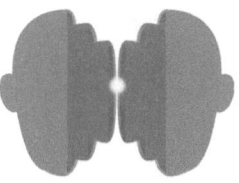

PART 2
The Cure for the Incurable

7

The Root Cause of Diseases of the B-MSY

When volcanoes erupt, they can spew hot, dangerous gases, ash, lava, and rocks. Various chemicals are thrown all around. The fire within the volcano is so hot that the surrounding land remains heated for several days, or even a few months!

The lava is not formed in a few days but is rather formed for many years under the earth's crust. The external and internal pressure on the earth forces many geological changes beneath the crust. The earth keeps absorbing the internal temperature of the core and the changes in the atmospheric factors. And one day, the pressure increases to such an extent that it causes a rupture in the earth's crust. The fire within bursts out and spreads around in the form of lava and chemicals. A moment before the volcanic eruption, everything seems so normal and peaceful. There are no warning signs, and suddenly, disaster strikes.

The same thing happens with our body. Pressure starts building in varied proportions within the body since our childhood. After being entangled in the illusory, sensory attractions and getting affected by the world, whatever thoughts and feelings are generated accumulate in the A-MSY in the form of positive or negative tendencies. The A-MSY tries to contain these tendencies as much as possible. But when the pressure of negative feelings and thoughts becomes excessive, it manifests as diseases in the A-MSY. Just like the volcano that erupts and spreads lava, if the diseases are not prevented in time, they manifest in the B-MSY and start affecting it.

If you want your B-MSY to always remain in optimal health, you must understand the root cause of all diseases and work on them to cure them forever. Healing disease at its root quickly leads you to complete health. Let's understand how disease enters the A-MSY to begin with.

1. Suppression of desires

The material world highly influences the five senses of the gross body, viz., the eyes, ears, nose, tongue, and skin. Due to ignorance and stupor, new desires arise within us every day while engaging in the world. "This should happen, that shouldn't; I want this, I don't want that, etc." These desires create stress within us. The stress, in turn, gradually affects our efficiency and creates turmoil within, which becomes a cause of disease.

When desires are gratified, they reinforce our belief that sense-enjoyments can satisfy us. We also develop the fear of losing what we have gained. When we are denied what we desire, it causes anger, anxiety, hatred, and sorrow. When we receive what we do not want, it causes hatred and aversion.

The role of the eyes is to see. But when we resist seeing certain things due to hatred or fear, this resistance gives an input to the A-MSY. And soon this affects our eyesight.

For example, consider scenarios where a relative has mentally harassed you, a friend cheated you in business, someone insulted you, you witnessed an accident, you spent your childhood in poverty, etc. These experiences trigger fear or hatred within you towards certain people or situations, and you do not want to see them again. These negative feelings program the A-MSY with the input that "I don't want to see clearly." Then illnesses related to the eyes emerge. They may cause blurred vision, myopia, asthenopia, and other visual disorders. This example illustrates how resistance, negative thoughts, and feelings that arise due to any reason can cause illnesses in the A-MSY, which later manifest as diseases in the B-MSY.

2. Suppression of negative thoughts

Our body is not trained to resist, but negative thoughts make us do that. Let's look at an example. A child performs well in his school. But one day, everyone mocks him when he answers in class. After that, fear sets in within him. He decides not to stand up and answer in class again. The thought "I do not want to stand up," starts affecting his limbs. Gradually his limbs become weak, or a disease leaves him impaired in the limbs!

Likewise, the fear of responsibility affects one's shoulders and wrists. Some people harbor negative thoughts continuously, which results in them reiterating negative affirmations about their health. So, their overall health begins to deteriorate.

3. Suppression of emotions

A negative thought, a feeling of hurt, or excitement can trigger various sensations in our body, which may be positive or negative. When we fail to manage these emotions or use them properly, they settle into various body parts in the form of diseases.

Those who harbor negative emotions like irritation, anger, hatred, and anxiety, fall prey to various disorders like acidity, migraine, heart attacks, hypertension, diabetes, backache, etc. Research has proven that anxiety about the future affects one's blood-circulation system. Consequently, his heart experiences a lack of joy. This, in turn, leads to heart diseases like heart attacks and high blood pressure.

Untoward incidents or emotions related to childhood memories often instill guilt in one's mind. He gets stuck in these hurtful memories and remembers them repeatedly. As a result, these poor memories create bondages within him. Such people can become victims of diseases like tumors, cancer, kidney failure, etc. People who get stuck in feelings of guilt suffer from depression, lack of enthusiasm, constipation, wrong habits, addictions, and backache.

Hence, we must understand that diseases are caused not merely due to external factors but also by the emotions we suppress within us. This is because we are neither sensitive towards these subtle sensations within the body nor habituated to understanding them. We get so overwhelmed by the thoughts, habits, and worldly cravings in our B-MSY that we fail to feel and acknowledge the A-MSY.

Imagine two radios set at different volume levels and being played simultaneously. We can only hear the louder one. Similarly, although the A-MSY has its own subtler vibrations and is at work at the same time as the B-MSY, the presence of the A-MSY gets dimmed in the grosser noise of the B-MSY. Therefore, it is necessary to balance our thoughts and feelings within ourselves besides balancing our life in the world outside. Else, they will continue to erupt and cause mayhem in the B-MSY while disrupting our poise and sensitivity towards the A-MSY.

We have understood the invisible mental effects on the subtle body. With this understanding, we can cure the root cause of every incurable disease and enjoy complete health in all spheres of the gross body.

8

Understanding the Nature of Diseases in the B-MSY and Their Cure

In the mythological epic Ramayana, the demon-king Ravana had ten heads. During the battle between Lord Rama and Ravana, the arrows shot by Lord Rama cut off Ravana's heads one by one, but they immediately grew back again. Finally, Lord Rama ended Ravana's life by shooting at his navel. Similarly, instead of curing each disease one by one, we should focus on attaining the complete health of the B-MSY. It can be fully cured only when our A-MSY is awakened again.

Our negative feelings, thoughts, beliefs, and desires disturb the A-MSY. However hard we try to get rid of them, they emerge again. Working on every thought and feeling is as futile as beheading Ravana's heads one by one as another negative thought or feeling will replace each one. Hence, we need to attack the navel, the root cause to get rid of them all at once. This attack is nothing but gaining knowledge of the truth.

The knowledge of truth improves our understanding of the A-MSY and works like medicine. For example, suppose you are diagnosed with a disease and contact a doctor for its cure. The doctor gives you some information, so your fears are immediately alleviated and you are convinced that your disease can be cured completely. Before meeting the doctor, you would have been anxious and afraid. But as soon as you speak to him, you feel better. Similarly, when we convey health-related understanding to the A-MSY, when the wisdom of truth is verbally communicated to the A-MSY, this wisdom acts like medicine and immediately starts curing the B-MSY. Let us understand this in detail.

1. Simple yet effective cure

People catch physical and mental diseases quickly in today's stressful environment, with extreme lifestyles and poor eating habits. They take the help of medicines to seek relief from these diseases and gradually become dependent on them.

Nowadays, many people suffer from knee pain and backache. They keep visiting doctors, but to no avail. Doctors recommend knee joint replacements, prescribe painkillers for quick relief, or advise them to undergo physiotherapy. However, the cure for such diseases is very simple. In fact, every disease can be easily cured.

For example, a person is suffering from severe backache. Someone advises him to correct his sitting posture, but he does not believe them. He consults many doctors but finds no relief. Finally, he gives up visiting doctors and brings about a small change in his routine. He takes an hourly break in the office, stands up from his chair, and bends his back backward for a while. He corrects his sitting posture on the chair. And soon, his backache diminishes.

These days, people often complain of abdominal pain due to unhealthy eating habits arising from sensory cravings for taste. The root cause of most illnesses is the stomach. Many diseases proliferate due to a poor digestive system. Diseases like stomach ulcers, acidity, constipation, diarrhea, and kidney stones are caused due to poor eating habits. People keep consuming medicines for many years to cure them. However, we can easily get rid of these diseases if we pay attention to our eating habits and bring about small lifestyle changes. This is an example of a simple yet effective cure.

2. The human body is continuously changing

Let us understand this with an example. Imagine that you are staying in a house where one brick gets replaced with a new one every day. In this way, after some time, all the bricks get replaced. The cement, beams, columns, and paint of the house also change after some time. This happens so gradually and subtly that you don't even realize it. So, even when the entire house has changed after some time, you still believe, "I am living in my old house."

Our physical body, the B-MSY, is like this house wherein old cells are dying and new cells are being generated every moment. The blood, skin, and even bones in the physical body are completely renewed with new ones over the years. Now, Science has also proven that every cell in the body is replaced. Then the question arises, "If everything is changing in the body, why does the disease still remain?"

Nature is doing its best in its rebuilding process by changing and renewing the body. Yet, we believe, "I am still the same old body with the disease." When these thoughts are repeatedly affirmed, they get reinforced as beliefs in our subconscious mind. The more evidence we acquire, the more we strengthen the belief. Effectively, a belief becomes an undisputed truth for us. These beliefs then perpetuate themselves in our daily lives by manifesting conditions that resonate with them. Our indiscriminate focus on the disease keeps it alive and makes it incurable.

People live with many so-called incurable, terminal, or chronic diseases. With the renewal of the cells, the disease should ideally have vanished from their bodies. The body that had the disease is no longer there. If nothing old remains, the disease should also vanish. The disease continues to exist in the body due to limiting beliefs held in the mind. These beliefs perpetuate themselves into new cells in the form of inherited cellular memories, causing the continuance of the disease.

What is the remedy, then?

The remedy is to release our limiting beliefs and inculcate progressive beliefs and healthy habits. We can achieve this by communicating with the A-MSY.

We need to build doubtless conviction in the following fundamental truths about healing -

- Diseases persist because of our limiting beliefs.
- Beliefs can be transformed at a deeper level.
- The A-MSY can restore the body's natural, healthy state.
- The A-MSY can be brought into action by invoking its abilities and instructing it to do so.

When we build conviction in this understanding, there will be no reason left for diseases to remain. The body in which the disease was present is no longer there. Affirm daily with conviction, "Now I have a new body. The effect of the old disease is no longer present. I am now free from the disease." Your conviction will help invoke the abilities of the A-MSY for healthy body renewal.

Once this simple secret is understood, then no disease will have a ground to persist. It will also allow your health to blossom. Of course, you must take the medicines prescribed by your doctor. But continuously conversing with your A-MSY can speed up the healing process, and soon, the treasure of health will be revealed to you.

3. The cure for every incurable disease lies within you

Every incident, thought, and illness has a cause, and where there is a cause, there is a remedy. If there is a problem, there is a solution. This is the law of nature. The solution to a problem is ready even before the problem arises! We may fail to decode it due to our ignorance.

Similarly, if you are facing problems or stress today, its solution must be already there within you, but you may fail to recognize it. Hereafter, whenever you face a problem, be it physical, mental, financial, social, or spiritual, try to seek the understanding to cure it from within you.

Incurable diseases cannot be cured with external remedies. It seems impossible to be healed from such diseases. People lose hope. But if they believe that "The cure for every incurable disease lies within me," this will work as a magical medicine.

A unique power exists within each of us, with which we can heal ourselves and be free of every disease. However sick any part of the body may be, the A-MSY always has a healthy blueprint of every body part. Hence, we can invoke the A-MSY to restore the healthy blueprint of any body part to the B-MSY.

Every part of the body is rooted in a subtle realm. Each part has its own A-MSY. The heart, lungs, eyes, arms, legs, back, and every other part of the body has an individual A-MSY. These small A-MSYs together form the A-MSY of the whole body. Every part has the ability to heal itself. We can converse with the A-MSY of each part and awaken its healing power. With continuous self-affirmation and praying to the respective A-MSYs for healing, we can help each part heal. This way, we can heal our whole A-MSY and in turn restore the health of the B-MSY.

If we aspire for a healthy, prosperous, harmonious life, free from all tendencies, with higher consciousness, we must learn the art of conversing with the A-MSY.

9

Communicating With the A-MSY for Healing Illnesses

Life is like an ocean. If we let it flow, positive energy in the form of divine love, bliss, peace, prosperity, and health flows freely in and through life. Even if some impurities enter life unknowingly, nature removes them on its own and purifies life once again. Animals and humans are gifted with this ability. Animals demonstrate it beautifully by healing themselves. However, humans cannot fully demonstrate it as they often become overwhelmed with stress, tendencies, and negative thoughts. This, in turn, poses hurdles in the free flow of positive energy. It affects life to such an extent that it shows up in the form of diseases in the B-MSY.

In such a situation, we can communicate with the A-MSY and awaken its latent powers for attaining good health.

It is important to have the utmost faith and complete surrender while communicating with the A-MSY, as our feelings play a vital role over our words. Therefore, regardless of the words we use for communication, we need to imbue faith, conviction, and complete surrender in our feelings, which will work wonders.

For example, consider your entire body is infested with an infection. It is not getting cured despite numerous treatments. You can communicate with your A-MSY using the following six steps and relieve yourself of the infection.

1. Invite and welcome your A-MSY:

   "My dear divine A-MSY, I heartily invite you into my field of awareness."

2. Communicate with the A-MSY:

   Depending on the nature of your B-MSY, you can communicate with your A-MSY differently.

   - If you are predominantly visual, while conversing with your A-MSY, visualize that divine white light is showered on your diseased body part and it is being healed.
   - If you are predominantly auditory, repeat the following positive affirmations and experience daily miracles in your health. You can also create positive affirmations for an individual body part and repeat them.
     - I am getting healthier with every incoming breath.
     - Divine energy is flowing through every cell of my body.
     - Day by day, my health is getting better and better.
     - I am healthy, perfect, and in full awareness.
   - If you are predominantly kinesthetic, gently touch the ailing part of your body with your hands and communicate with it. You can thank and bless it.

3. Seek forgiveness from the A-MSY:

   "Dear A-MSY, I indulged in wrong tendencies and poor eating

habits. I ignored a balanced diet, proper food intake, and exercise. I harbored negative thoughts and feelings for people. I hankered after futile desires. This has built pressure on my body parts, making them ill. The body had to suffer. Please forgive me for my ignorance.

"To date, I have not paid enough attention to my life. I have been carried away by the lure of the senses. I have considered others inferior to me. Owing to this behavior, I am unhealthy and restless today. Please forgive me for that."

4. Assert and request the A-MSY to get into action:

"Dear A-MSY, please use your healing powers and free me from this illness. You have all the powers to heal my ailment completely and make me disease-free. Please begin your healing process and bestow complete health upon me."

5. Chant and send the A-MSY out of your field of awareness:

Close your eyes for some time and repeat a mantra, positive affirmation, or chant the words love, joy, and peace. Love, joy, and peace are divine qualities. They can heal every ailment and restore the original, healthy state of the body.

After some time, request the A-MSY to leave your field of awareness by saying, "Dear divine A-MSY, please continue to heal even after leaving my field of awareness. You may now leave my field of awareness."

6. Express gratitude:

Thank your A-MSY by saying, "I am grateful to you for coming into my field of awareness and supporting me. Thank you… Thank you… Thank you…"

7. Slowly open your eyes when you experience a pleasant feeling. Have complete faith that your illness has been cured; it is just a matter of time before it begins to manifest in the B-MSY.

You may communicate with your A-MSY in your own words.

Once you understand this cure, your illness will not have the grounds to survive, and your health will blossom. Additionally, you may consult a doctor and continue taking prescribed medicines. But this knowledge will help you heal at the earliest.

Communicate with your A-MSY in the same manner as two intimate friends openly share and have complete faith in one another. You can communicate with the A-MSY of your entire body or that of any specific, ailing body part.

Let's understand how we can briefly communicate with the A-MSY of a body part. Imagine you are experiencing severe pain in your upper back. This is how you can briefly communicate with your back's A-MSY.

1. "Dear divine A-MSY of my back, I respectfully invite you into my field of awareness. You are most welcome!
2. I am experiencing health-related miracles every day.
3. I have time and again neglected the health of my back, so I seek forgiveness from you from the bottom of my heart.
4. I have complete faith that you can heal my backache. I assert that you have all the powers to help me heal. Please help me. Please begin the healing process."
5. Close your eyes and chant for some time. Love, joy, and peace...

   "Love, joy, and peace are helping my back heal. Love, joy, and peace can cure any illness. Love, joy, peace... Love, joy, peace... Love, joy, peace...

Communicating with the A-MSY for healing illnesses

> My dear A-MSY, you may now leave my field of awareness. Please continue to heal even after leaving my field of awareness.
>
> 6. Dear divine A-MSY of my back, I thank you for your unconditional support. I will always be obliged to you. Thank you… Thank you… Thank you."

The upper backache is just an example. Similarly, whatever your illness, like diabetes, heart ailments, kidney problems, issues with your eyes, etc., you may seek optimum health with the help of your A-MSY. Believe it! Many people have attained miraculous results with the help of this prayer in all five planes of their lives.

Testimonial - 1

Going From Illness to Wellness - The Magic Wand

When birds and animals fall sick or suffer from a physical injury, they quietly isolate themselves for some time and allow nature to heal them or consume naturally available medicinal herbs to cure their disease. This happens naturally and intuitively with them. Nature has also bestowed the same power to the A-MSYs of human beings. But very few know about it.

Many seekers have received the knowledge of A-MSY communication through Sirshree's discourses. They have practically applied this knowledge and reaped benefits in their lives. The chapters on Testimonials share some of their experiences so that you can build conviction in the powers of the A-MSY.

> "Since childhood, I was fragile and prone to illnesses due to the negative feelings that soaked me. However, when I heard about the A-MSY prayer, I began working with it and experiencing several miracles in my life. The results reinforced my faith to such an extent that I am free of most medications today. For the slightest of ailments in my body, I immediately communicate with my A-MSY. This has

Testimonial - 1

almost healed all my ailments like frozen shoulder, tennis elbow, and varicose veins.

Besides this, the doctors diagnosed that my muscles had weakened, leading to the displacement of the uterus and urinary bladder. They recommended an emergency surgery. All pre-operative tests were carried out. Only the date of the surgery had to be finalized. The estimate for the surgery was about Rs. Two Lacs.

At that time, I got the intuition from within to continue with the existing medication for some more time instead of going ahead with the surgery. We decided so.

Since that day, I started praying to my A-MSY several times daily. I would visualize my body brimming with health just as before. Along with the medication, I continued communicating with my A-MSY for an entire year. I would pray even during my walks after dinner.

In my next check-up, it was found that the uterus muscles had exceptionally strengthened. The doctors were surprised and declared that there was no need for the surgery.

In this way, whenever I suffer from major or minor illnesses, I use the magic wand of the A-MSY, and my health is restored in no time."

Lalita Swakul

***

This experience unfolds a new dimension of healing wherein, along with communicating with the A-MSY, we can also experiment with our power of visualization. Just as Mrs. Swakul visualized herself brimming with complete health, you, too, can visualize yourself with a new dimension of health.

In fact, with A-MSY communication, sometimes we encounter situations where we meet a good doctor or dietician and benefit from their consultation.

Let us look at one more experience where the disciple cured her ailing body part with the help of the A-MSY of her other body part.

> "I used to always suffer from abdominal pain. Whenever I would dine out or have a change in my diet on visiting some place, it would upset my stomach. Despite treating myself with many remedies, I could not locate the root cause of the problem. Then, I took help of Sirshree's teachings and experimented with A-MSY communication. For a few days, I only communicated with my stomach's A-MSY.
>
> Then from one more discourse of Sirshree, I learned that the disease should be eliminated from its root. A new aspect of the stomach's A-MSY unfolded before me that the food reaches the stomach via the tongue, and until the brain wishes, we don't feel like eating. This means our brain and tongue are responsible for making food reach our stomach.
>
> Since then, I also started communicating with the A-MSYs of my brain and tongue. I prayed to them, "Dear A-MSYs of my brain and tongue, please support my stomach's A-MSY. Please give me the right hints for a healthy diet. Together the three of you can do it. Thank you… Thank you… Thank you…"

Bharati Masurkar

***

With this experience, we understand that we can take the help of the A-MSYs of other body parts to heal the diseased body part. For example, if you are suffering from knee pain, you can seek help from your hand's A-MSY by inviting it into your field of awareness. Tap your knee lovingly with your hand as if you are caressing a child. Then pass on energy and love to your knee through your hands.

Similarly, you can also take the help of the A-MSYs of your head and heart. All the body parts inform the brain about their aches and pains, and the brain, in turn, signals them to work accordingly. You can invite your brain's A-MSY into your field of awareness and seek its help for the best coordination in the process. You can also take the help of your heart's A-MSY for ideal blood circulation in the body.

In this manner, we can eliminate any disease or problem from its root. Remember, you are not advised to adopt only this method without seeking a doctor's treatment. Use this magic wand of A-MSY communication along with your prescribed medication from your doctor and experience complete health for yourself.

10

Conversing With Other Peoples' A-MSYs

Imagine how ecstatic you feel when you heartily gift someone with something! Just doing something for someone also makes you feel reassured, and your mind blooms with unknown happiness. This joy augments when the other person reciprocates your gesture with a return gift.

These days people feel happier when they receive a return gift after attending a function, a birthday party, an anniversary party, or a wedding. This is a social norm. Some people follow it while some do not. It depends entirely on their will. But, when you pray to God for someone's health, prosperity, or success, you indeed receive the return gift from God in the form of divine blessings! This is 100% certain.

Today, it has been scientifically proven that whenever we think about someone, whether it is something positive or negative, our vibrations reach that person. And unknowingly, that person returns the same vibrations to us. This happens in the invisible realm. So, although we cannot see it, we can definitely feel it.

Conversing with Other Peoples' A-MSYs

You may have also experienced that sometimes you feel good after meeting someone, whereas sometimes you don't feel like talking to someone. Why does this happen?

The reason is obvious. The other person doesn't feel good about you. Hence, good feelings do not arise within you for them. On the other hand, sometimes, you feel so intimate upon meeting someone that hours spent with them seem like minutes to you. This is the magic of vibrations! Vibrations of two people reach one another regardless of whether they are nearby or miles apart.

If vibrations can work wonders, why not use them to attain good health for people? If along with your health, your dear ones' health is also at its best, it will only add to your life!

Yes! We can invite other peoples' A-MSYs into our field of awareness and communicate with them about their health. This will increase their possibility of becoming healthy. When we perform any work selflessly, nature supports us completely, and the result of such work is truly positive.

Let us understand this better with an analogy.

> Ramesh was out of town on an official assignment. After completing his work, he met Raj Verma, his old college friend, at his house. It was a long time since they had last met each other. Raj's family members were happy to see Ramesh after so many years. All of them were reminiscing the old moments they had shared together. Suddenly, Mohan Verma, Raj's father, started experiencing pain in his chest. He began sweating a lot. Soon, he fell unconscious. Everyone was perturbed.
>
> Until the ambulance arrived, Ramesh offered first aid treatment to Mr. Verma with a calm and composed mind.

Since Ramesh was aware of A-MSY communication, he also communicated with Mohan Verma's A-MSY and prayed to it.

Ramesh invited Mr. Verma's A-MSY into his field of awareness and asserted:

"Dear Mohan uncle's divine A-MSY,
I invite and welcome you
into my field of awareness.
I respect you. I am fond of you.
You have the power to heal any ailment.
You can heal this heart ailment.
Whatever be the reason why the free flow of
blood has stopped in your body,
you have the power to heal it.
You can bring the blood flow back to normal.
Please clear all the arteries where there are blockages.
Please start the healing process and
continue your magical healing.
Thank You... Thank You... Thank You..."

This way, Ramesh went through all the steps we learned earlier. Throughout the day, he continued the prayer whenever time permitted him. Mohan Verma's health began to improve in two days! A relieved Raj shed tears of joy as he embraced Ramesh. All the family members breathed a sigh of relief and heartily thanked Ramesh for the timely support.

If someone in your family or neighborhood falls ill, you can pray to their A-MSY to heal them. An ailing person often feels so weak in such circumstances that he cannot pray for himself. It could be because he is not in the state to pray, or he might not be aware of the power of the A-MSY, or may not have faith in it. In such circumstances, you can communicate with his A-MSY and seek help for his healing.

In fact, you can pray for everyone who comes into contact with you and is not feeling well. They could be miles apart from you and you cannot physically reach them. Yet, instead of panicking, you can invite their A-MSY into your field of awareness and request it to heal them. The distance doesn't matter because whether it is your A-MSY or someone else's, it is capable of reaching anywhere.

Our prayers also reach other peoples' A-MSYs. It works like medicine, assertion, and blessing for them, and their A-MSY starts healing itself.

Healthy people should take responsibility for universal healing. If God has blessed us with abundant health, it is our responsibility to heal the entire world! For this selfless cause, thousands of seekers at Tej Gyan Foundation pray together at 9:09 pm daily. Mass prayers have remarkable power. They bring about miraculous results. You, too, can participate in this prayer. You can read about it in detail on the last page of the book.

Testimonial - 2

Be Instrumental in Healing Others

In today's world, it is very easy to communicate with our loved ones within minutes, whether they are close by or miles apart. But this communication is limited to the physical level only.

The previous chapter has revealed yet another secret! You can also communicate with other peoples' A-MSY, their subtle body. Consider that an ailing person is struggling with pain. The thought of communicating with his A-MSY doesn't even occur to him, or maybe he is unaware of this knowledge. In such a situation, when someone prays for him, communication begins between his A-MSY and that of the person praying for him since we are all essentially connected in oneness as the same Self (God, or Consciousness). Therefore, external medication, prayers, and affirmations reach the ailing person's A-MSY, and his A-MSY starts following the healing instructions it receives. As a result, his body starts healing. Some seekers have applied this understanding in their lives. Let's look at their experiences.

Dr. Kanchan Nagarkar's son developed a sudden problem in his left eye and he couldn't see anymore. Along with seeking treatment from an ophthalmologist, she learned the art of conversing with her son's A-MSY and started doing so regularly. She saw miraculous results within only a few days! Let us read more about her experience.

"I had an amazing experience with the A-MSY prayer. My son suddenly stopped seeing with his left eye one day. We immediately consulted an ophthalmologist. All his reports, including the CT scan, were normal. Then we visited a neurologist. He examined my son and told me that the nerve in his left eye was inflamed. This is known as optic neuritis. However, he neither mentioned the cause nor the time it would take to heal. He said it might take six months or even a year or two to recover. Then along with the doctor's medication, I decided to pray to his A-MSY regularly.

Every day, I would invite the A-MSY of my son's left eye into my field of awareness and pray -

'You have the power to heal yourself.

Together you, me, and all the

Masters of Part One and Part Two

can heal the diseased all over the world.

The nerves of the eyes are strengthening themselves

with the power of love, joy, and peace.

The right eye is supporting the left eye in healing.

You can see everything, near and far, clearly.

So, please start healing.

Continue healing even after you leave my field of awareness.'

Meanwhile, the doctor started injecting him with steroids. I also started praying that these medicines should have only a positive effect on him. After ten days, when we visited the doctor for a checkup, he was surprised to see my son had regained fifty percent of his vision! After fifteen more days, my son could see everything clearly. He was completely healed.

The doctor then tapered the dosage of his medicine and stopped all medicines in three months. I have witnessed such profound evidence of the power of the A-MSY prayer that now I am no longer afraid of any disease. We have our own doctor within us."

Dr. Kanchan Nagarkar

When you communicate with someone else's A-MSY and request it to make the person healthy, nature also supports you by letting the healing vibrations flow all around. As a result, the level of your consciousness also rises along with that of the diseased person. This way, you can seek the help of many masters simultaneously for universal well-being.

***

Masters are advanced souls who operate from a higher level of consciousness for the well-being of all. Some masters are in Part One, i.e., on earth, while there are masters also in Part Two, i.e., beyond earth, who help heal people on earth. The entire world can be healed with the support of these masters.

Hence, you are not on your own! You can seek the support of these masters to help others. When you seek help from the A-MSYs of the masters in Part One and Part Two, they attune themselves to people's subtle bodies and attract things as per your prayers or create a basis for incidents to happen accordingly. All A-MSYs are connected with each other in the same way as electric poles are connected with each other by wires. Hence, you can seek help from the A-MSYs that are attuned and aligned with each other. Let's understand this through another seeker's experience.

> "I am a gynecologist. A woman in her eighth month of pregnancy visited me. She had diabetes. Her blood sugar level was above 380. She started experiencing labor pains in the eighth month itself. As an emergency, a caesarian delivery was required. On examining her, it was found that her condition was critical. It was not that easy to operate on her.
>
> Under normal circumstances, I take the help of only one assistant while doing the Caesarian procedure. But the lady was so overweight that I had to take the help of three additional assistants. The baby's weight was around four kilograms. The baby was stuck in the womb. The fat of both the mother and baby was so much in excess that I found it impossible to get the baby out. In those days, I was reading Sirshree's rendering of the Bhagavad Gita. I came across a line that said whenever in trouble, one should meditate. Then problems or troubles subside without affecting us internally. I, too, had a dire situation. I paused for a while and called out to God deeply, 'Help… Help… Help… I can't take this anymore. I am helpless. Now you have to manage this.' Then I prayed to my A-MSY, 'You can successfully complete this surgery. Please complete it!' And then the baby was safely delivered!
>
> We saw a big blue mark on the child's right shoulder. The other doctors said, 'It seems difficult to heal this arm.' Then

I remembered my treasure. I communicated with the baby's A-MSY, 'You have divine power within you. You can heal yourself. Awaken your divine power and heal your arm.' I visualized divine healing white light on the baby. And within two days, the miracle happened! The baby began to move her arm and the color of the skin returned to normal. The mother also recovered completely. All the doctors were astonished to see this miraculous result. I thanked God from the bottom of my heart."

(A Gynecologist)

11

Communicate To Be Healthy Forever

Whenever you adore and respect elderly or honorable people, they mostly bless you, saying, "May your life be always filled with happiness, good health, success, and prosperity." It means that you are happy now and will always be happy in the future. You are healthy now and will be healthy forever. Always keep progressing from whatever situation you are in.

Every person wishes to progress in his life by being healthy and happy. For that, in addition to putting in his best efforts, he must communicate with his A-MSY to lead a smooth, peaceful life, and also attain the highest purpose of his life.

You may wonder, "When I am fit and fine, why do I need to communicate with the A-MSY?"

A-MSY communication is not only meant to heal diseases but also to attain supreme health. One considers himself healthy if he is not suffering from any disease. But this is not so. One can be considered at the pinnacle of health when along with not having any diseases, one's efficiency, immunity, life-force, zeal, and vigor are at their peak. One can take advantage of A-MSY communication to achieve this.

Following are the steps to communicate with your A-MSY to reach this supreme state of health.

1. "My dear A-MSY, I invite and welcome you into my field of awareness."

2. Communicate with the A-MSY about what you want:

    - For better efficiency: "I want to experience a constant flow of energy throughout the day to heartily complete all my tasks on time. Let my body go beyond its comfort zone and always be energized. Let every part of my body be healthy and support me. Even if it faces any problem for any reason, may it develop the capacity to heal itself."

    - For keeping every part of the body healthy: "Let every part of my body be blessed with optimal life-force. Let it always be fit and healthy. Day by day, my health is getting better and better. I am healthy. I am fine. I am awakened. Help me heal the A-MSY of every part of my body. Help the subtle bodies of all body parts, right from my head to the toe, so that they remain healthy and support me. Please help improve my immunity."

    - For seasonal health issues: "May every change in weather affect my body only positively. May it help to improve my health. May the external changes not negatively influence my gross body but support it in every way. Wherever you are, whatever the environment you are in, adapt yourself to it, and adjust yourself to the atmosphere."

        Similarly, you can communicate with your A-MSY for any other requests, too.

3. "To date, you have always kept me healthy, supported me a lot, and guided me in doing all my work at every turn of my life. But I have never thanked you. Please forgive me for this."

4. Assert with faith, "You have all the power to help me attain the supreme state of health. You can make this happen. Please start your work."

5. "I now allow love, joy, and peace to rejuvenate my life-force. Love, joy, peace… Love, joy, peace…" Chant this for a few moments.

    "Please continue your support even after leaving my field of awareness."

6. "Thank you for coming into my field of awareness and conversing with me."

Thus, the subtle body can be made healthy with the combination of prayer and meditation.

Often one gets overwhelmed by stress, tendencies, and negative thoughts and unknowingly poses hurdles in the free flow of love, joy, and peace. Although one may not see any immediate blocks in his life due to this, he needs to keep conversing with his A-MSY and experience love, joy, and peace to avoid any future blocks. Then, nothing can stop him from dwelling in divine health.

Testimonial - 3

To Help Maintain the Treasure of Your Health

People often doubt when they invite their A-MSY whether it really comes into their field of awareness.

We must understand that the gross body can never see the subtle body. In the motorbike-car analogy, the car can never see the motorbike as the motorbike is connected to the car from within. Similarly, the A-MSY is connected to the B-MSY from within.

Instead of checking whether the A-MSY has come into your field of awareness, patiently continue with the A-MSY prayer. The results you see will be all the proof you need! Many people have experimented with this and experienced miraculous results in their lives.

We will consider one more such experience where the person is completely healthy and enthusiastically carries out her daily activities. Yet, she communicates with her A-MSY daily to seek its support to maintain this healthy state even in the future. It ensures that she can carry out all her activities smoothly until the end of her B-MSY and she progresses in every sphere of life.

"I am Bindu from Pune, India. I am blessed with perfect health. I easily let go of all the troubles of my life with a smile. I pray to God, 'If you have given me this problem, you will only solve it. Please show me the right path and give me the right understanding so that I understand what you want to do and take the right steps in life. You alone are going to do it. My body is only a medium.'

Believe me, everything happens perfectly in my life and only for my highest growth. When I heard Sirshree's discourse on A-MSY, I thought, 'Since I am absolutely healthy, why should I communicate with my A-MSY?' And I got the answer that I am healthy today, but what about tomorrow? The B-MSY will show signs of deterioration with time. So, it is better to start praying from this moment itself, "Please keep supporting me with good health even in the future so that my body remains active until its end." Thereafter, with this understanding, I started communicating with my A-MSY daily.

1. 'O, my divine A-MSY, I invite and welcome you into my field of awareness.

2. You have supported me completely to date. You have kept me healthy, physically and mentally. You have helped me have loving relationships with everyone and strengthened me to move forward with them.

   You have also fully cooperated with me to make progress in my life. Even in the journey ahead, may my A-MSY and B-MSY together help me stay healthy in all aspects of life. This is also your responsibility.

3. If, knowingly or unknowingly, any part of my body is unwell due to my carelessness, please forgive me, and support me in healing it.

4. You have the power to dwell in this grace forever. May all the parts of my A-body and B-body function smoothly.

5. Let all the parts of the body be healed with love, joy, and peace.

   Please continue your support even after leaving my field of awareness.

6. Thank you… Thank you… Thank you…'

My day starts with the A-MSY prayer, and my B-MSY remains energetic throughout the day!"

Bindu Ahuja

Similarly, if you start communicating with your A-MSY daily, even an undiagnosed disease within you, in its initial stage, will get healed before it becomes symptomatic! Even if a disease shows the slightest symptoms in the B-MSY, it will be treated immediately and healed in time.

12

Essential Qualities To Gain Effective Outcomes

Whenever we hear something unconventional, we don't believe it immediately. The same thing happens with the idea of A-MSY communication. Since people do not see anyone practicing A-MSY communication, they doubt whether it really works.

When such doubts arise in your mind, it impacts the effectiveness of your A-MSY communication and you do not get the desired outcome. But when you contemplate the shortcomings of your A-MSY communication and work upon them, you can get a better outcome.

Let us understand the essential qualities you must have or develop for an effective outcome.

1. Faith

Imagine that you want to buy a shop and need money for that. Whom will you ask for help? Obviously, you will borrow money from a friend or relative who can lend it and you are confident they will help you.

Similarly, you must have faith in your A-MSY that it has the power to give you what you want. You have to express this faith through your communication. You must set aside all the baseless doubts and assert complete faith in your A-MSY. Only then can the A-MSY bring miraculous results in your life. When you have complete faith in someone, it brings only positive results!

Positive evidence will deepen your faith and deepened faith will strengthen your assertion, which will further add to the effectiveness of the outcome. This will help catalyze the process.

Yet, at times, doubts arise in one's mind, "What if my prayers are not fulfilled?" Or even after praying for healing, he is uncertain about it and keeps complaining to his friends and acquaintances about his aches and pains. He does not realize that by saying this, he has, in turn, strengthened the feeling of distrust in nature. Hence, be careful not to give space to the slightest negativity in your thoughts and speech.

2. Receptivity

When you communicate with your A-MSY with complete faith and chant love, joy, and peace, you actually surrender all your problems to the divine power and the A-MSY. Thereafter, you must raise your receptivity so that the solutions to your problems or the desired results start moving toward you. When you become completely receptive, nature starts working for you.

For example, when you place an order for something online, you eagerly wait for its delivery. You try and stay at home all the time to receive it when it arrives. Similarly, when you ask your A-MSY for health, prosperity, success, and harmony in relationships, and if you are not open to receive it, how can it reach you? Hence, ensure that you are receptive to the results of your prayer.

3. Awareness

You have to develop enough awareness within yourself that if you encounter the slightest problem in your life, you can immediately communicate with your A-MSY to resolve it.

Negative feelings, sorrow, or any changes in your body immediately warn you that something is going wrong or that you may fall ill. This is the law of nature. If you are unaware of it, the disease or problem takes root within and you come to know about it only after it aggravates. Hence, be aware of the slightest changes and keep communicating with your A-MSY.

At the same time, be aware of where the solution to your problem is coming from. For example, when you communicate with your A-MSY to heal an illness and consistently work on medication, assertion, and prayer, the A-MSY starts working immediately. You may then observe some thoughts and feelings arising within you. You may suddenly meet someone who may share the information you need to cure your illness. You may find out about a good doctor from someone. You may think of making changes to your diet and so on. This way, nature will guide you in one way or another. All you need is the awareness to catch these signals and become aware of them.

For example, you have a sore throat. You face difficulty in swallowing. Suddenly, you may come across a video with a recipe for making hot decoction, and you may strongly feel, "Yes, let me try it!" What is this thought? This is nothing but the cure to your illness conveyed to you in the form of thoughts.

You must catch this signal. But here, one often makes a mistake. He thinks, "I have communicated with my A-MSY. That's it. Now miracles will happen on their own!" But this is not always so! You have to be aware of the signs nature sends.

4. Consistency

Consistently communicating with your A-MSY alone begets success. You may question how long you have to practice this. The answer is you have to practice it until you get the result or you are satisfied.

Practice A-MSY communication at least twice a day to ensure consistency. You can do it after waking up in the morning and before going to bed. In the morning, you are calm and peaceful after being connected to the Self throughout the night. Hence, when you communicate with your A-MSY in the morning, your A-MSY will keep an eye on your routine throughout the day and you will remain aware.

Your body undergoes healing and repair while you are asleep at night. Hence, whenever you communicate with your A-MSY at night and consistently pray for healing, the ailing cells also get repaired along with general healing. Consistent communication reinforces the A-MSY and it serves as a reminder for you.

5. Concentration

Whenever you work on something, you need to be completely focused on the task. Only then will you get your desired results. If your attention wanders, your thoughts are unstable, or your mind is troubled, you will not be able to communicate with your A-MSY properly. Hence, keep your communication brief but ensure that it's precise and clear.

Brief communication does not imply changing or cutting down the essence of your communication. It means you should communicate your intention in fewer words and quickly resume your work.

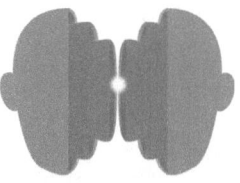

PART 3

Sending Vibrational Energy

13

Enliven Your Relationships

There was a time when Jay and Vijay, two brothers, could not live without each other, even for a moment. They lived in adjoining houses sharing a common courtyard. The love and brotherhood shared between their families set the role model of an ideal family for everyone around them. Everything was fine until their children grew up. As the children grew older, their relationship gradually turned sour. This was because Jay's sons were brilliant in studies and excelled in all other fields, while Vijay's sons were average and passed their exams with great difficulty.

Because of this, the seed of jealousy began to grow between the two families and soon, it grew into a big tree of hatred. A high wall was erected between their courtyards and they only transmitted negative thoughts upon seeing each other. Even if they didn't say anything directly, their negative vibes affected each other.

This has become the story of every household today. Discord between families, sour relationships, competition with each other based on their standards of living and their children's performances, and estrangement over petty issues have become very common. Sometimes, even outsiders are dragged into family disputes.

One of the primary reasons for the increasing bitterness in relationships is negativity in thoughts toward people. When we harbor a bad feeling for someone, that negative energy reaches the other person. This subtle transaction of feelings happens in the unseen. People feel that only their spoken words reach and influence the other person. But in reality, the energy of our thoughts also reaches the other person's A-MSY, regardless of it being negative or positive!

After knowing this, your responsibility increases manifold. If something similar is happening in your family or with your acquaintances, you need to start sending positive energy called "Winergy" to everyone while remaining neutral toward them.

"Winergy" leads to a win-win situation where both sides win. Thus, winergy is "win-win energy!"

By sending winergy through your words or thoughts, you send positive energy to others' A-MSY and raise their consciousness. As a result, a surge of positive energy flows among everyone and you also benefit from it.

We must consciously use only positive affirmations in this communication. After inviting the other person's A-MSY into our field of awareness, we should assert:

"You are pure and complete. You are the essence of God. You are virtuous, righteous, and dear to me. You can never commit a mistake. Whatever has happened or is happening is because of some wrong belief. May God forgive both of us. Our relationship is getting sweeter day by day and brimming with love and affection. Together, our families are serving everyone's greater good. God bless you; God bless me; God bless everyone. Let the world be blessed divinely."

To sum it up, you can say, "You are DEAR. You are always there. You are special to me."

Here, DEAR = D+E+A+R. 'D' stands for Divine, 'E' for Essence of God, 'A' for Affection, and 'R' for righteousness. You assert this to the A-MSY, the person's higher consciousness, not their body.

So, when you send winergy to someone, its effect begins showing. The winergy you transmit enlivens you more than the other person. If they send negative energy to you, it affects you negatively, too. However, the winergy you send forms a protective shield around you, so no negative energy enters your space.

When there is discord in relationships, sending winergy is beneficial for everyone. Sending winergy makes relationships beautiful. If someone harbors hatred for you, winergy nullifies its negative effects on you. If someone is thinking about you vehemently, its negativity does not impact you. Every impending negative situation is smoothly dissolved before it reaches you with winergy. Benevolence prevails both in your life and that of others.

Healthy relationships empower you to attain success in every sphere of life. The harmony and sweetness in relationships lead you to progress toward the ultimate purpose of your life. With A-MSY communication, you can make your relationships sweet and robust.

We have been blessed with different relationships in our life on earth so that we can learn our life lessons with their help and attain the purpose for which we were born. But instead of treading the path of love, goodwill, and cooperation, we get into conflict, comparison, and the blind race of superiority complex, leading to bitterness in our life. Sometimes, we even think of leaving those relationships and moving away from the world, but we fail to do so. As a result, we suffer grief, disappointment, and mental stress, leading to various diseases in the physical body.

The relationships that could have served as a ladder for our progress and filled our life with love become the cause of our downfall. It is important to understand a few things to strengthen our relationships so that the A-MSY prayer brings about positive results in our B-MSY.

Let us understand these things and add some new dimensions to our life.

1. Everyone, knowingly or unknowingly, seeks love and appreciation. They want everyone to love and give importance to them. But the law of nature says that when you give love to someone, they will also love you in return. The plant will grow only when you sow the seeds in the ground. The crop cannot grow without sowing the seeds. Hence, when we take the initiative and start showering love upon others, we will also start receiving love. After knowing this secret, you will not wait to receive love and respect from people, but you will begin giving away love. Whether someone gives you a flower (blessing) or not, you start giving away flowers to them.

2. Relatives are our messengers. By making them instrumental, nature fulfills our prayers and desires. Sometimes an idea, thought, or message is sent to us through them. Hence, the better our relationship with people, the easier it will be for us to receive signals from nature.

3. In ancient times, people used to go to the Himalayas or forests to conquer their vices and tendencies and purify themselves by undergoing penance for years. But today, you don't have to go anywhere. Rather, the world around you will serve as a

ground for your penance. Only by staying amid the world can you learn to live with love, harmony, and brotherhood. This understanding will inspire you to make your relations healthy.

4. One often commits a mistake in relationships. He thinks, "If only the other person changes, my life will be wonderful. Let my in-laws change… let my son start obeying me… let my spouse improve, and so on." The truth is that people don't change, but relationships do deteriorate. We must understand that people are our mirrors. Looking at them, we have to do our makeup, not theirs. We have to improve ourselves. Once we change, they will change automatically.

5. Many times in relationships, we blame others, but we hurt ourselves more than them. If we contemplate on this, we will see that the other person vented his anger and left, but we keep hurting ourselves by remembering that incident repeatedly. No one can hurt you if you don't want to be hurt. But in ignorance, one keeps hurting oneself by repeatedly reiterating past incidents.

Now with this new understanding, stop hurting yourself and work toward raising your consciousness. Besides yourself, give winergy to others and work toward raising their consciousness, too. All you have to say to everyone's A-MSYs is, "You are DEAR. You are pure. You are filled with love, bliss, and faith."

Love, bliss, and faith are qualities that make one perfect and complete. Everyone's consciousness, or true Self, is always perfect. It is full of love and bliss. You are only glorifying its qualities. You aren't saying anything wrong because your A-MSY and those of others are full of divine qualities. You are admiring these qualities. This will bring about transformation in your life and fill it with love and bliss.

14

Have Faith in the Boatman

Ashok used to be happy and cheerful always. He shifted to live in a new neighborhood. He befriended everyone with his broad smile. He would strive his best to help anyone in difficulty. He would treat everyone as his dear one and talk to them. His face always radiated a glow. As he was not financially well-off, people wondered about the secret of his happiness.

Seeing him happy always, his neighbor, Naresh, couldn't hold back his curiosity anymore and finally asked, "Hi Ashok! While everyone seems to suffer from some confusion, anxiety, or disease, how come you are always happy? There must be ups and downs in your life, too!"

Ashok replied with a sweet smile, "It is normal to have ups and downs in life! If you are journeying somewhere by boat, the boat is bound to sway at times. There will be storms amid the otherwise gentle weather. But if you have complete faith in the boatman, there's no place for fear or worry!

"We are sailing in the boat of life in the worldly sea. Since we have come to earth, we are bound to see the ups and downs of life. Nobody has ever been spared from this. Amid this, if we are connected with our Source and seek help from the A-MSY to lead us in the right direction, then come what may, we can see only positive aspects in every incident. Because whatever is happening is as per the divine plan of nature for our holistic growth!"

Naresh was a bit upset after hearing this and said, "It is normal to have some ups and downs in our life and we can strive our best to overcome these situations, too. But when one toils hard day and night for himself and his family and receives only disrespect, disregard, and taunts in return, he loses all enthusiasm in life. Life seems like a burden for him. How can he be happy then? Thinking about growth is farfetched for such an unhappy person!"

"Yes," Ashok replied, "But sometimes nature doesn't show results the way the mind expects. Sometimes, the results can be more beautiful than what is expected. Sometimes, a prayer remains unfulfilled or takes long to be fulfilled. In such a case, have faith that the non-fulfillment is happening for your good only. If you are destined for a comfortable and safe life as per nature's divine plan, your prayers will bring you everything in abundance, but not so much that it leads to your downfall. Nature bestows everyone with what they need after considering their best interests."

Suddenly, Naresh shared in a serious tone, "I work so hard for my family but they don't appreciate my efforts. Instead, they consider me ambitious and belittle me using bitter words. Ideally, this shouldn't happen. It makes me feel lonely and depressed!"

Ashok consoled Naresh, "Those who function by communicating with their A-MSY, need not worry about anything because they carry out every deed considering it as a deed of God!"

Naresh enquired, "How can we establish a smooth connection with our A-MSY, and how do its results come about?"

Ashok then revealed, "Consider your A-MSY as your close friend. When you invite it into your field of awareness with complete faith, communicate with it lovingly, and inform it about your problem, it will help you. Our A-MSY fully supports us in bringing harmony in relationships, developing mutual understanding, and interacting lovingly with each other. When we consistently converse with the A-MSY, we soon see miraculous results in life."

Naresh decided to communicate with his A-MSY and headed home. He experienced an unprecedented bliss within him.

That day when he retired to bed after finishing his work, he communicated with his A-MSY. He said:

1. "My dear divine A-MSY, I invite you into my field of awareness. Please come to my field of awareness. You are welcome.

2. My dear divine A-MSY, may I share a bond full of love with my dear ones. May everyone understand my feelings and acknowledge my love. May my dedication to my family be recognized. May I receive the right appreciation so I can happily carry out my responsibilities.

3. To date, you have immensely supported me, but I have never even thanked you. Please forgive me for that.

4. I assert that you have the power to make my life blissful. You can make this happen. Please start working on it.

5. The power of Love, Joy, and Peace can help you in this endeavor. Please allow love, joy, and peace to help you."

After that, Naresh chanted, "Love, Joy, Peace," for a few minutes. He concluded his communication by saying, "Please continue your cooperation even after leaving my field of awareness. Thank you… Thank you… Thank you…"

With a deep feeling of gratitude, Naresh slowly opened his eyes.

After that, Naresh consistently communicated with his A-MSY as and when he remembered during the day. In a few days, he observed a change in his family members' behavior. He heartily thanked his A-MSY and his loved ones for this change. A-MSY communication then became a part of his life.

When we connect with the A-MSY and seek its help, everything begins to flow freely in our life. We need to have unwavering faith, so that our negative thoughts and resistance do not pose hurdles in the joys flowing toward us. Instead of living life assuming ourselves to be the doer, if we surrender to the Will of God, then what is in line with our life's purpose will automatically flow toward us.

Testimonial - 4

You are Pure and Flawless

Sometimes, family quarrels leave a deep scar that seems almost impossible to heal. At times, the cause of these quarrels is the stubborn ego of people who are reluctant to budge. The impact of these quarrels is seen to be passed from one generation to another. Even if only one sensible person stands on either side, he will try to resolve the conflict. But how can he do it? Let's understand how a seeker dealt with the conflict so that it got resolved itself.

"It was June 2020. My cousin's marriage was fixed. That was the year of lockdown due to the pandemic. Apart from the outside lockdown, everyone in our family had their minds closed to each other for the past few years. Our mental lockdown started when my grandmother passed away in 2015. After that, our relationships were strained due to mutual discord.

Earlier, the families of my two maternal uncles, my aunt, and my mother, always enjoyed together. Since childhood, I have received boundless love from all of them. I was troubled by their strained relationship. It seemed my uncle would get my cousin married without the presence of our three families. Then I invited my uncle's A-MSY into my field of awareness and sought forgiveness from him. I said, 'You are pure. You are the higher consciousness. I love you. You also love the entire family very much.'

After that, I put this prayer in the prayer box of our house, 'Akshay's marriage will bring happiness in the family like before and I will be able to receive the childhood love from all my relatives.'

After three days of my prayers, my uncle surprisingly transferred some amount into the accounts of all my relatives! He called and told us, 'Start shopping for the wedding in your respective cities. We will solemnize the wedding within 15 days with 50 members.'

After a long time, the entire family was reunited! Everyone thoroughly rejoiced. I felt like my childhood had returned and I was dancing with joy. This miracle was possible only due to the wisdom received from Sirshree! He has imbibed in us the importance of the power of prayer and the power of faith."

Swapnaja Jadhav

***

So, when we start sending winergy to others, miracles happen for sure. The only purpose of sending winergy is to transmit positive energy to the other person's A-MSY. You communicate with their higher consciousness and remind it of its divine qualities like "You are divine. You are pure. You are holy." This means that the higher consciousness dwelling in their B-MSY is always flawless and full of divine qualities. Many times others, too, wish the same. When you communicate with their A-MSY in this manner, they also reciprocate in the same manner. Thus, both parties win. This is a win-win situation where no one is inferior or superior. This way, an unresolved conflict gets resolved effortlessly!

Winergy is a positive energy that can be passed on to anyone, regardless of whether you know them personally or not. This can also be effective at a mass level. For example, if two countries are at war or there is a stressful situation between some countries, you can send winergy from your A-MSY to the leaders and people of those nations and pray for their peace. Even a small positive thought you have can help change situations.

Along with this, you can also communicate with your A-MSY. Whenever any adverse events happen in the world, such as theft, burglary, atrocities against women, epidemics, or natural disasters (droughts, floods), you can practice A-MSY communication. At such times, while following all the steps of A-MSY communication, you can invite your A-MSY into your field of awareness and assert, "My dear divine A-MSY! I dearly love you. I respect you. Please be stable and calm, and work for human welfare."

You may think, "If someone else is doing wrong, why should I communicate with my A-MSY?" The truth is that everyone's A-MSY is connected in the background! When we communicate with one A-MSY, it affects others, too.

You can invite your A-MSY into your field of awareness and communicate with it not only for untoward incidents but also for good events. For example, when the crop is good, scientists have invented something new, or some policy is launched for the welfare of the poor, then communicate with your A-MSY, "My dear A-MSY! You did a great job; keep up the good work! It's really wonderful! Thank you... Thank you... Thank you..."

Testimonial - 4

As you start practicing this, you will be surprised to see that whatever you communicate with your A-MSY is getting communicated everywhere and its results are also reflected everywhere. This way, the A-MSY prayer can be used to change the social mindset, protect from any pandemic, elevate social morale, and much more in every sphere of life. As you experiment with it yourself, your faith will deepen. Likewise, when you appreciate and express gratitude to the A-MSY for the good work it is doing, this feeling also gets transmitted to the collective A-MSY, which promotes collective positivity. Now you can understand the multiple benefits of the A-MSY prayer.

***

When you want to do selfless work and there is fear or dilemma in your mind about whether the "work will be done or not," the A-MSY prayer proves very effective. If you communicate with the other person's A-MSY before meeting them, then besides your message, positive energy also reaches them to complete your work. A-MSY communication is a universal remedy that enables such selfless work.

Let us read through the experience of another seeker who communicated with her manager's A-MSY and resolved the difficulty at her workplace.

> "I worked at the Public Works Department (P.W.D.), a government office. I wished to organize a 'Stress-free Life' program for all the department staff. But it was known that the officer from whom the official permission was to be taken was strictly against such programs. But, I had so much faith in Sirshree's teachings that I decided to talk to him despite this.

I was supposed to meet him at 10:30 am the next day. Everybody believed that he would reject the proposal.

The next day at 9:09 am, along with the collective prayer for world peace offered at Tej Gyan Foundation, I prayed to the officer's A-MSY with complete faith. I invited his A-MSY into my field of awareness and communicated, 'This retreat is not being organized to earn money but for a selfless cause. Please cooperate with us.' I thanked him with faith that the program was completed.

When we met him at 10:30 am, it was surprising that after listening to us for only two to three minutes, he not only praised our work but also gracefully granted permission to organize the retreat. Moreover, he sent an official notice for conducting this program to all the offices of the department. Within the next four days, the program was organized for about two hundred and fifty members of our staff."

Savita Lele

15

Children Are Little Bosses; Grownups Are Big Bosses

Rajesh was seething with anger when he stepped out of his boss Keval's cabin. "What's going on is sheer dictatorship! I don't know what he thinks of himself. No matter how well I perform, he always finds mistakes. He lacks humanity. God knows why he is always so upset with me! I always reach the office on time and sincerely complete all the work assigned to me. But look at Shirish - of the eight hours at work, he invariably spends a couple of hours in the cafeteria gorging on snacks and chatting. He hardly completes his work on time. And yet, he gets to be the boss's blue-eyed boy. They get along so well. Just look at the way Keval has humiliated me today. I would enjoy the spectacle if only he, too, were to put up with such humiliation. It will cool the embers of the pain he has put me through."

Like Rajesh, many believe that people don't reciprocate even though they complete their office work and fulfill their household duties with great sincerity. Such people only focus on their work and ignore the feelings and thoughts they carry for other people. They think action is more important than feelings. They assume that whatever opinions or feelings they harbor for others are not visible. Hence, they try to be good to others but think negatively about them behind their backs. The truth is we have a sweet and heartfelt relationship with only those people for whom we feel and think positively.

In the above example, if Rajesh wants to improve his relationship with Keval, he can do so by sending winergy to Keval's A-MSY, seeking forgiveness, and focusing on his highest qualities. For this, he needs to invite Keval's A-MSY into his field of awareness and communicate this way:

1. "Dear Keval's divine A-MSY, I invite you into my field of awareness. You are welcome.

2. Your intention behind pointing out my mistakes yesterday was for the company's betterment. But I took it personally, overreacted, and used inappropriate words. I was deeply hurt by the derogatory comments you made to me out of anger. I always focus on your negatives and hence I always judge you wrongly. But hereafter, I will try to focus on your virtues.

3. Due to our argument, I abused and cursed you in my mind, for which I sincerely apologize from the bottom of my heart. In a fit of anger, I wished for you ill, blamed you, and pointed faults in you. Please ignore everything and purge it from your heart. May God forgive both of us.

4. Dear Keval's divine A-MSY, I have forgiven you, and I know you have forgiven me too. Now, let's start a new relationship on a sweet note. We can do it. Hence start working on reconciling the relationship.

5. Good luck be with you… Good luck is with you… Good luck is always with you… You can now leave my field of awareness.

6. Please continue your support even after leaving my field of awareness. Thank you, Keval."

When Rajesh communicated with Keval's A-MSY in this manner, Keval's behavior changed toward him within a few days and they started supporting each other.

We encounter some situations every day where we cannot directly communicate certain things to our relatives and friends, and withhold them. Let us consider circumstances where we can convey our point to the other person's A-MSY using A-MSY communication.

Communication with children about their education

Parents often feel that what their children are doing can have bad consequences. They want to guide their children in the right direction but the children are not ready to listen to them. They believe, "We have grown up. We don't need anyone's advice or opinion." This leads to arguments between the parents and children, which sometimes results in quarrels in the family. This strains the relationship further. The children were willing to listen to some advice earlier but now become adamant and refuse to listen to anything. The parents worry about how they should get their children to understand. In such a case, they can converse with their children's A-MSY. Direct communication with their A-MSY is very effective when the children are asleep because that's when the mind is the most calm and receptive. Let's understand how a parent can communicate with their child's A-MSY. Let's assume the child's name is Shekhar.

1. "My dear Shekhar's divine A-MSY, I invite you into my field of awareness. You are welcome.

2. You are engrossed on your mobile phone even while studying. This habit impairs your concentration, learning ability, and

quality. Your friends who tempt you to play mobile games are not your true friends. They lack direction and are leading you astray. True friends are those who guide you to walk the right path.

3. You have the understanding to choose the right friends. So, choose the right friends. If you learn to make the right choice at every turn of your life, you will always be happy and successful.

4. All the masters of Part One and Part Two are supporting you in making the right choice."

In this manner, follow all the steps and complete the A-MSY communication.

Communication to dispel depression

Rita's younger sister Mahi was a victim of depression. She would look at every incident from a negative perspective. She was undergoing treatment and yet the situation was not under control. She would frequently have suicidal thoughts. Everyone in the family was concerned and anxious for her.

Many of us have people in our families who are consumed by negative thoughts and suffer from emotional imbalance. Their emotional upheavals also affect the harmony and peace within their families. Due to their neurotic condition, their level of consciousness is often low due to which they cannot receive any direct guidance from the people around them. However, if we communicate with their A-MSYs consistently, it can bring about a change in their understanding and disposition.

Rita can practice such a prayer for Mahi:

1. "My dear Mahi's divine A-MSY, I invite you into my field of awareness. You are welcome.

2. You are sacred; you are the essence of divinity. Love, joy, and peace are your innate nature. You are the creator of your thoughts. If you can choose to be sad, you can also choose to be happy. You can be happy every moment because happiness is your true nature.

3. You can eliminate the thoughts that bring sorrow and anxiety within you. You have the power to change the wrong beliefs that you have harbored in you, knowingly or unknowingly.

4. So, please put an end to all the sad feelings. Erase all the deep-rooted beliefs in your mind and fill your life with positive thoughts. You can do this. Start working on it.

5. Please allow love, joy, and peace to work wonders in your life. Love, Joy, Peace… Love, Joy, Peace… Love, Joy, Peace…

   My dear Mahi's divine A-MSY, you may now leave my field of awareness. Please continue to heal even after leaving my field of awareness.

6. Thank you… Thank you… Thank you…

Thus, if you want to communicate something to someone, start communicating with their A-MSY first. Besides this, before going to bed every night, ask yourself, "Whom did I hurt today?" If you have hurt someone, knowingly or unknowingly, it should come to light. Only then can you invite their A-MSY into your field of awareness, communicate with them, seek forgiveness, and heal the bitterness in your relationship in time to bring back the sweetness into it. This daily practice will help you harmonize your relationships. This is an invisible law of nature that operates by itself. No one can change it.

16

Conquering Behavioral Patterns With Inner Strength

In today's world, one faces several challenges. Along with their mindset, their social framework has also changed completely. In such a situation, they face problems related to health, livelihood, strained relationships, global warming, and the deteriorating impact on the nutritional value of food items due to an impure and polluted environment. These problems affect their health adversely. When one's B-MSY is unwell, a negative train of thoughts keeps racing in their mind incessantly. As a result, they always remain in a stressful state and their inner strength weakens. A life full of love and joy merely remains a dream for them.

- Is living your entire life under such stress and discomfort a true way to live?

- What should we do while living life so that along with health, all other problems of life are also resolved?

- How should we control a racing mind so that it starts obeying us?

To get rid of these problems, start communicating with your A-MSY and exercising its powers. This will make your mind Steadfast, Obedient, Untainted, and Loving, which is the SOUL purpose of your life. Along with your health, your inner strength will increase, and your relationships will also be strengthened. Gradually, as these qualities develop within you, all your deeply ingrained beliefs, behavioral patterns, wrong habits, and tendencies will also come to an end.

Let's learn a few types of A-MSY communication, and adopt them so that we can inculcate those qualities in our life.

Communication for liberation from behavioral patterns

Each person has different types of tendencies, i.e., deep-seated patterns of behavior. Some have a tendency of fear, some of anger; some are overwhelmed by lethargy, and yet others by ambitions. Some get entangled in sensory cravings and some are caught in the grip of an inflated ego. Some struggle with confusion while some lack enthusiasm. Practicing A-MSY communication can help get rid of all these tendencies. To attain our goals, we can take the help of the powers of our A-MSY by giving it medication, assertion, and winergy. We can do it using the following steps:

1. "My dear divine A-MSY, I invite you into my field of awareness. I welcome you.

2. I have many tendencies, habits, and beliefs that frequently lower my consciousness, due to which, fear, anger, lethargy, and attachment overpower and distract me from my goals. Then the feelings of guilt and regret arise and a vicious cycle begins. Today, I want complete freedom from all my patterns, tendencies, habits, and beliefs.

3. To date, I have lived my life with these patterns and beliefs. I have faced many problems because of them that have slowed down my progress. I haven't paid attention to this at all. Please forgive me for that.

4. I assert with faith that you have all the powers that can liberate me from this. Please remove these patterns, tendencies, and habits from my life and help me walk the path of progress."

5. Now, close your eyes and chant, "Love, Joy, Peace," for a while.

   "My divine A-MSY, please continue your work even after leaving my field of awareness.

6. Thank you... Thank you... Thank you ..."

Communication for gaining inner strength

Inner strength is the most important kind of strength. It helps you progress in all areas of life. Whether you want to control your senses or win over your tendencies, inner strength helps you succeed. Hence, pray to your A-MSY to gain inner strength first.

1. "My dear divine A-MSY, I invite you into my field of awareness. I welcome you.

2. I want to master my senses. They must never distract me from my goal. Even if such a situation arises, my inner strength should win over my sensory cravings and tendencies, and guide me so that I leave no stone unturned in progressing toward my goal. Let my inner strength be more powerful than my tendencies so that my inner growth can happen easily. May my inner strength never falter amid the illusory world and may it always remain high.

3. To date, I have hankered after satiating my sensory cravings and in the process, I fell prey to many wrong habits and tendencies

unknowingly. But I never paid attention to these tendencies. Please forgive me for this.

4. You have all the power to boost my inner strength and I assert with faith that you can work on it for me. Please start working on it."

5. Now, close your eyes and chant, "Love, Joy, and Peace," for a while. Then request your A-MSY to leave your field of awareness.

6. Communicate to your A-MSY, "Please continue your work even after leaving my field of awareness. Thank you very much for everything. Thank you... Thank you... Thank you..."

Communication for cultivating divine qualities

The mind should be steadfast, obedient, untainted, and loving to attain the goal of inner growth. On the spiritual path of transcendental progress, one needs to have patience, faith in the unseen, and the attitudes of acceptance, witnessing, and surrender. You can communicate with your A-MSY for imbibing the divine qualities of love, joy, peace, creativity, courage, and honesty.

1. "My dear divine A-MSY, I invite you into my field of awareness. I welcome you.

2. Please bless me with all the divine qualities necessary for my progress. May qualities like courage, confidence, love, patience, righteousness, forbearance, tolerance, and health become integral to my personality. May I give love to everybody and receive it from others freely. May I interact with everyone lovingly. May I succeed in every sphere of life — physical, mental, financial, social, and spiritual.

3. To date, I have not paid attention to my qualities or worked on my concentration. Whenever I started working on something,

my mind would get bored quickly and I would leave the work incomplete. I never worked on myself. Please forgive me.

4. I know that you have the power to sculpt all the qualities within me. Please help me stay focused amid all the worldly temptations. I have complete faith in you and I am sure you can do it."

5. Please close your eyes for some time and chant the mantra of your choice.

    "My divine A-MSY, you can leave my field of awareness now. Please continue the work of elevating my qualities and concentration to greater heights even afterward.

6. Thank you… Thank you… Thank you…"

If you aim to attain the pinnacle of inner progress, you can consistently communicate with your A-MSY with awareness to keep your level of consciousness high. This will free you from all the patterns, tendencies, or habits that hinder your journey toward your goals.

Testimonial - 5

Gaining Liberation from Tendencies

Many people have deeply ingrained tendencies that trouble not only them but also others who live with them. They undergo such grave physical and mental suffering that others can't help them even if they want to. The people around them feel helpless and regretful. They may think, "We are helpless. We, too, are suffering along with him. God knows what bad karma we have incurred that we must endure this."

But this book is now guiding you. Have faith; whatever problems you may face, be it someone's health, getting rid of certain habits, or overcoming your tendencies, instead of being scared, you can seek healing through A-MSY communication. Even if it is a baby, their subtle body has the power to know and understand everything. A-MSY communication can help you heal any mental illness, habits, and tendencies for yourself and others.

Let's read about an experience where the child has a mental illness and is living a life of stupor.

"My son, Vaibhav, suddenly suffered from depression in 2009. He began losing his temper easily. In a fit of rage, he would even break household items. He believed, 'Dad and mom don't love me at all.' He would always threaten to put an end to himself. He would call me a 'wicked mother.' He would also quarrel with his sister and beat her. He had become irritable. He would not study and always demand new things. 'I want a dog, a cat, a fish tank right away.' Sometimes he would ask for food items. 'I want a pizza, a burger right now.' It had become difficult for the four of us to live together under the same roof.

We consulted a doctor and began his treatment. Considering his behavior, he was undergoing counseling once a week. We got completely involved in his treatment and our whole life revolved around him.

In the same year, we received a write-up on A-MSY communication from Tej Gyan Foundation. We considered it as a prayer and felt so happy as if all our problems had come to an end. We started performing the prayer regularly.

Every morning and night, we consistently performed the A-MSY prayer for five years. We would wake up at five or six in the morning and invite the A-MSYs of Vaibhav's brain and heart into our field of awareness and communicate with them. At night after he would sleep, between ten and eleven o'clock, we would perform the prayer again, from the bottom of our hearts with complete faith.

The A-MSY prayer changed his life completely. The medication and counseling went on for five years. Later, we stopped it as per the doctor's advice. After that, we continued with the magic wand of the A-MSY prayer only. Now, the A-MSY prayer has become an integral part of me. Vaibhav has also become completely healthy and mature. He has become very calm and looks after our entire business."

Bharati Maluvade

***

Some deep-rooted tendencies may take time to break because the other person may not be receptive to the healing power you radiate and understand you. In his stupor or due to his tendencies and habits, he builds a shield of resistance around himself which blocks the healing prayers from reaching him. The prayers will heal him for sure. But first, pray to raise his receptivity so the healing prayers can start working on him.

Prayers work faster for people who are aware and open to receiving them. If the one you pray for is receptive, i.e., there is an alignment between the receiver and the giver, then the results are quick and effective.

The same applies to your own A-MSY as well. If you have some deep-rooted tendencies that do not dissolve easily, your senses also entangle you in them. In that case, you can communicate to that part of the body where the senses have deepened that tendency and free yourself from it

For example, if you are addicted to junk food due to your taste buds, then invite your tongue's A-MSY and assert, "O divine A-MSY of my beloved tongue, please don't get entangled in eating junk food. Please help me stay healthy." If you pray this way, the process of transformation will begin.

Likewise, if you have the tendency of laziness or fear, you can pray to your A-MSY to get free from it and remain energetic in all situations. Let's understand this with the experience of another seeker.

"I had a phobia of hospitals, operation theatres, and doctors. The tendency of fear was so strong that even if the doctor asked me to get a simple test done, I would be overwhelmed with negative thoughts, nervousness, and insomnia. Since I heard about the A-MSY prayer from Sirshree's discourses, I started practicing it regularly to get freedom from this tendency.

One day, due to a sudden fall, my leg was fractured. The doctor advised me an urgent operation. I immediately started praying to my A-MSY, not for healing my leg but for liberation from the tendency of fear and anxiety.

I prayed, 'My dear A-MSY! Please dwell in the feeling of acceptance and surrender. Let God's will be my will. You have the power to end my tendency of fear that separates me from God. Respond according to the understanding you have attained from Sirshree's discourses.'

With this prayer, I witnessed a miracle. Earlier, I would be afraid of getting a simple blood test done, but now I was undergoing a major operation, yet there was no fear or anxiety. I was immersed in a state of complete calmness. I thought, 'It takes years of rigorous penance for people to get rid of their tendencies. But we have been blessed with such a simple and powerful tool.' Now, I am convinced that anything is possible with the A-MSY prayer. Thank you!"

Anju Maheshwari

17

A-MSY Communication for Emotional Maturity

Two friends devoted themselves to the social cause of eradicating poverty and illiteracy. They traveled to many villages distributing food, clothes, and essential medicines to the needy. They explained the importance of education to the villagers and encouraged them to send their children to school. They started this work with the intention of public welfare. They would feel happy seeing smiles on the faces of the poor. Gradually, they became famous among the villagers, and their work was appreciated. Then they started an NGO and received a generous contribution from the wealthy toward this noble cause.

One of them was swayed by the name and honor they received, and his feelings began to change. He started longing for more fame and considered keeping a part of the donations for himself. He got overwhelmed with the feeling of earning more and more fame and money instead of giving genuine service. Although he would assert, "I am working for the poor," he inadvertently started harboring greed and guilt.

Our feelings work at such a subtle level that, knowingly or unknowingly, we become oblivious to them. The situation worsens when we get carried away by our negative feelings, make wrong decisions, and engage in useless arguments with others.

Since we're unable to handle our negative emotions, we often lose our ability to discriminate between right and wrong. This is the state of emotional immaturity.

For example, a mother lashed out badly at her daughter because she skipped school to watch a movie with her friends. When the mother came to know about it, she couldn't control her anger and started screaming and scolding her daughter. The mother didn't know why she got so charged. Was it because of the daughter's lie or some other reason?

The daughter also got upset. She was overcome with anger and hatred. She murmured, "Mom just needs a reason to burst out at me. I wasn't alone. All my friends were there. Now I have grown up. But she considers me a child even now. I have to seek her permission to do anything. I can't do anything of my free will. I need to become her slave and always obey her commands. Now I won't talk to her."

The mother had different thoughts in her mind. "When children grow up, they follow their own will and don't understand how much the family worries for them. They go anyplace without informing us."

Nowadays, such incidents are common in and around our homes every day. These little fights trigger many feelings that get suppressed because people do not know how to handle their emotions properly. This is due to a lack of emotional maturity.

Anger, distress, and worry are superficial feelings that can be easily perceived and understood as negative feelings. But many other subtle feelings never come to light. Hence one never realizes them. For instance, when one is overpowered by boredom, he spends hours watching TV in futility and then regrets, "Why did I waste so much time!"

To escape their negative feelings, some people spend hours shopping in the mall. They end up wasting money purchasing unnecessary things. Some burst out at their family members or strangers when their wish is not fulfilled. Some spend long hours chatting mindlessly with their friends on the phone or in person. With this, they feel relieved of their negative feelings, but it is only for a short time. Soon the negative feeling recurs. All these ways of escaping emotions indicate emotional immaturity.

An emotionally mature person knows how to make best use of his time. Instead of spending hours watching TV, he enjoys reading books or doing productive work. He uses his money effectively, and plans and invests his finances well. He contemplates how his emotions affect his relationships and uses his words thoughtfully.

Emotional maturity is essential for a happy and peaceful life. Then alone can one say that his life is successful. One can attain this maturity at any point in life. Whatever your age now, you can communicate with your A-MSY and request it to help you master your feelings and raise your emotional maturity.

Let's understand how to communicate with your A-MSY for this purpose with the following steps:

1. "My dear divine A-MSY, I invite you into my field of awareness. I welcome you.

2. To date, you have been associated with me and patiently witnessed all my emotions—good or bad, right or wrong,

anger or anxiety, hatred or jealousy. You acted according to my feelings without saying anything.

Today, when I gain this wisdom to understand my feelings and improve them, please help me control them. Please guide me in increasing my emotional maturity so that I have harmonious relationships with everyone and can support one and all in every sphere of life.

3. Please forgive me for all the trouble I've caused you due to my mindlessness. Please forgive me for all the suffering you had to undergo because of my ignorance and immaturity.

4. I need your complete support. And I assert with faith that you can do it.

    I want to express divine qualities in my life. May my life be filled with love, joy, and peace. May all my decisions arise from a mature mindset so that it has a positive impact on the lives of others."

5. Invoke, "Love, Joy, Peace."

    "Please continue your support in mastering my feelings even after leaving my field of awareness.

6. Thank you… Thank you… Thank you…"

18

Sending Your Messenger by Saying What You Want

Everyone knows about Lord Rama's war against the demon king, Ravana, in the Ramayana. Lord Rama possessed immense powers and had mighty warriors like Hanuman, Angad, and Sugriva by his side. If he had wished, he could have directly gone on the offensive against Ravana's army. Yet he sent Angad as his emissary before the war to make a peace treaty. He didn't want any loss of lives, any harm to mankind, or the devastation of any family. It was a situation of a great war for the triumph of truth over evil. Yet, by sending a messenger of peace, he chose harmony!

Times have changed now. There is discord in almost every home. A strong feeling of jealousy and hatred is taking root in peoples' hearts. Everyone is embroiled in an internal war. A cold war is going on in so many households. In such a situation, very few people take the initiative to end the war and welcome peace. People keep shooting invisible arrows of thoughts and feelings at each other and do not want to leave any stone unturned to demean each other. To resolve this situation and maintain love and peace, sending a peace messenger to the other person is essential, but that thought does not occur to everyone.

These days, even though we do not have powerful messengers like Hanuman and Angad, we all have a great, powerful A-MSY capable of acting as our peace messenger.

Yes! Our invisible subtle body, our A-MSY, has all the powers to reach anywhere instantly and communicate our message to others' A-MSYs without saying a word.

You may have heard about astral travel or remember the information in the first section of this book. When one is asleep, his subtle body travels out of his gross body. Some people have attained occult powers through spiritual practice and can journey anywhere with their subtle bodies at will.

Then why not use our subtle body positively as a peace messenger? You may wonder, "Why should I take the initiative when the other person doesn't even think about it?"

The answer is that you alone have to take the initiative because this book is in your hands. It is a testimony to the fact that you are a friendly person and want to elevate your consciousness. You wish to have love, brotherhood, and peace in your relationships.

Let us first understand why we should send a messenger and how it will work for us.

By now, we have understood that we can communicate with someone else's A-MSY by inviting it into our field of awareness. But now we need to send our A-MSY as a messenger for peace talks to the other's A-MSY. We have to send the messenger before the actual scene arrives and communicate everything we want to say or explain to him at the meeting beforehand.

Suppose you want to crack a big deal with a big company and you come to know that you don't share a good relationship with the officer who will be finalizing the deal. If you have doubts about his decision, then send your A-MSY to him before the meeting and communicate everything you intend to tell him on meeting him.

You will say, "Dear divine A-MSY of …… (the officer's name), I have honestly sent my quotation to your company. I have quoted the lowest rates. I want to share a good business relationship with your company and provide you with high-quality goods /services at a lower rate. I assure you that the quality of the goods will be superior. You will have no room for complaints. If you trust me and finalize this deal, I will be pleased to work with your company. Thank you… Thank you… Thank you…"

When you repeat the same sentences in the meeting the next day, you will see the officer more agreeable with you because you have already convinced him of high-quality work through your A-MSY. In this way, your peace messenger communicated your message to him in advance and completed your work peacefully. Later you didn't have to convince him much. This is the magic of your personal peace messenger.

Likewise, when you are about to meet someone, and you feel that he may not respond properly, first send your peace messenger to him in advance so that it can create a platform for open communication. You need not follow all the steps in this communication. Only the two steps of conversation and gratitude are enough. But use correct and sensible words in your communication.

Many times, one sends a war messenger or rejection messenger by mistake. He communicates all negative things to the other person, not directly but through his thoughts. Similarly, people also send war messengers to us by thinking negatively about us.

In both cases, you should send your peace messenger only, especially if someone has sent a war messenger for you. This will not only save you from the negative impact of the war messenger but will also convey a message of peace to the other person.

When you play, you get hurt and also feel pain. What do you do then? You just ignore it, let go of it! Though it's hurting you, you ignore it and continue playing. Similarly, you must ignore the war messengers sent by others and keep sending your peace messenger to them. You cannot stop others from sending war messengers to you. They may also send rejection messengers as per their understanding. They may think negatively of you. But you must ignore those negative feelings and send your peace messenger only.

19

Communicating With Our Ancestors' A-MSYs

Be it life on earth or the afterlife, one can dwell in a balanced and contented state only when one has attained completeness.

No one likes incomplete topics, tasks, or conversations because they don't feel contented. For example, if you visit a hill station and spend all your time commuting and eating without visiting the important places there, then you feel incomplete. Some people feel incomplete when they visit a place of worship and don't perform any rituals. Some people feel incomplete if they are unable to speak their heart openly to someone.

Communication is a means of achieving completeness. It not only helps to eliminate doubts and misunderstandings from one's mind but also makes one's mind clear and pure. If you are unable to communicate with someone's gross body directly, you can take the help of the A-MSY prayer and communicate with their A-MSY to attain completeness. Each of us is gifted with the A-MSY prayer to eliminate any incompleteness in our life.

But what if someone's loved one dies and he regrets, "Now, I will never be able to talk to him. I wanted to say a lot to him. All those things remained unsaid and incomplete now. How can I attain completeness with him?"

The same is possible with our ancestors who may feel incomplete due to not being able to communicate some things during their earthly life. Many times, they left, causing misunderstandings among their relatives. For example, they went to Part Two (the subtle world/ afterlife) without properly dividing their property among their children. As a result, their children kept fighting with each other over the property. Sometimes the ancestors failed to express their love for their children. Or they left with some hurtful feelings without expressing them in words. So, they feel incomplete even when they're in Part Two.

There is life even after death. All our family members and relatives who passed away into Part Two are living there with their A-MSYs. They are not visible to us just because they are operating at different frequencies, but we can still communicate with their A-MSYs. For example, when they were with us in Part One, we may have had a rift with them, we may not have liked some of their words or deeds due to differences in opinions, and they too may not have liked some of our aspects. It is natural for this to happen while living together. But in case of some people, when their loved ones pass away and go into Part Two, they regret all their life, "I didn't behave well with him. I never appreciated him while he was living with me. I always threw tantrums due to my temper," and so on.

On the other hand, sometimes, the ancestors, who went to Part Two, may have misbehaved and hurt us. Hence, we harbor negative feelings for them. Sometimes, we carry the burden of these feelings throughout our life. With A-MSY communication, we can converse with their subtle bodies and be liberated from the burden of guilt and regret forever, as well as eliminate our negative feelings for them. Let's consider an example.

Radha suddenly lost her mother due to a heart attack. This news left her deeply shocked. The sorrow of this loss and the guilt of having misbehaved with her mother in the past troubled her. The whole movie of her life kept repeating in front of her eyes. She realized for the first time, "My greatest benefactor, my best well-wisher is no longer with me." She started recollecting all the good qualities of her mother. Now, she began to feel guilty, "I never admired her qualities, never valued her presence, never thanked her, never spent enough time with her, and never tried to understand her feelings." These thoughts left Radha in tears. She continued to experience the burden of guilt and regret many times a day for a long period.

Since Radha was unaware of an afterlife in Part Two, she didn't know that only her mother's B-MSY had perished, but her A-MSY still existed; she could converse with her A-MSY even now. If Radha had known that she could attain completion by communicating with her mother's A-MSY, she would have received the remedy to her sorrow. If she had received the knowledge about the A-MSY prayer, she could have practiced it this way.

1. "My dear mother's divine A-MSY, I invite and welcome you into my field of awareness.

2. I respect you. I love you. Dear mother, I am very much indebted to you. You loved me unconditionally, always supported me when I needed it the most, and guided me in the right direction. You patiently dealt with all the problems in life. The taste of the food you cooked can never be found elsewhere.

3. I realize the value of your presence now. Please forgive me for letting my rage take over and hurting you. Please forgive me for all my mistakes. May God forgive both of us.

4. May you receive true wisdom from God and dwell among people with a higher consciousness. May you be forever filled with the divine qualities of love, joy, and peace.

5. Please continue your beautiful journey even after leaving my field of awareness.

6. Thank you… Thank you… Thank you…"

The guilt and regret that the relative may experience for his deceased one may be experienced by the deceased, too. In Part Two, one gets a glimpse of his entire life on earth, just like a movie playing in front of his eyes. He regrets not behaving well with his parents, spouse, siblings, and so on, and engaging in unnecessary conflicts with them. He recollects how many times they had to bear his anger. He realizes he did not do the right thing. In such a state of mind, he stops progressing with his further journey in Part Two and keeps suffering in the flames of guilt. Though he wants to seek forgiveness, he can't do so. In such a situation, his relative on earth can communicate with his A-MSY to alleviate his pain and motivate him to progress on his journey.

1. "My dear _____(name of the relative)'s divine A-MSY, I welcome you into my field of awareness.

2. Please don't harbor any guilty feelings in your mind.

3. I am neither hurt nor sad by any of your actions. Please forget all the differences we had. I have forgiven you from the bottom of my heart. Now you are free with my forgiveness.

4. Now shift your attention toward your divine journey ahead. Don't worry about us, and don't carry any guilt, either."

5. Chanting of Love, Joy, Peace…

"You are brimming with new energy. Now, you are relieved of

a big burden. I thank God for this grace.

You can now leave my field of awareness.

6. Thank you... Thank you... Thank you..."

Often, we get to know about the death of a distant relative or acquaintance. Since we are not close to them, we may not feel very sad about it. But we feel like doing something for them. In this case, we can communicate with their A-MSY and share the understanding of the truth we have received with them. For example, a person lost his distant uncle. He can communicate with his uncle's A-MSY as follows.

1. "My dear uncle's divine A-MSY, I welcome you into my field of awareness.

2. I respect you. There are many great masters in the subtle world to give you higher guidance and support. Please seek their help and move ahead on your journey. Leave all earthly worries behind. Start your further journey with the understanding that you are not the body. Join the company of people with a higher consciousness and start contributing to the highest creation from the Source.

3. If you have any rifts with anyone, please forgive them.

4. Now, embark on your further journey with your subtle body. Love, joy, and peace are helping you move ahead."

5. Chant Love, Joy, Peace... Love, Joy, Peace...

   "You can now leave my field of awareness.

6. Thank you so much for listening to me."

Likewise, whenever you remember your relatives who have transitioned into Part Two, or you experience guilt, regret, or other feelings toward them, you can communicate with their A-MSY.

Testimonial - 6

Conversing with the A-MSY in Part Two

Everyone wants to have a loving relationship with everyone in society. He wants his family members, friends, neighbors, and colleagues to have a harmonious relationship. But sometimes, some situations lead to conflicts. Then they stop talking to each other despite their will, and their relationship becomes a formality. In such a situation, even if you intend to suggest or say something positive, people do not take it in the right spirit. Sometimes, a family member passes away suddenly, leaving you feeling shattered! You feel guilty, "I wish I could have told him the truth or shared my point of view with him."

Besides this, you may be going through certain incidents in your life for which your ancestors may have been responsible. For example, a court case regarding family property started many years ago and those ancestors passed onto Part Two, but the case is ongoing even today. Or an ancestor passed onto Part Two without making a will for his property, and the heirs are fighting among themselves today. You are unable to explain your point of view to anyone and feel suffocated. What can be done in such a case? How can you communicate with them? Let us read about one such experience.

"My father-in-law died in 2015. Thereafter, I used to feel that something was missing and would become restless. I had heard from Sirshree's discourses that everyone's journey is about a hundred years on earth, called Part One, and the latter journey in Part Two, if imagined in earthly terms, is about ten thousand years. Sirshree explained this journey in detail. We have always heard that one changes one's body like clothes after one's death. This means one continues his further journey in Part Two. With this faith, I invited my father-in-law's A-MSY into my field of awareness daily and sought forgiveness. I sent him healing rays and highlighted his qualities one by one through contemplation. Every morning, I used to pray to God. While doing so, I began to converse with his A-MSY, too. I communicated with him about his further journey and every small rift we had, every subtle thought I had about him, and attained completion.

Moreover, I received some indications that made me feel that he has blessed me and said, 'Dear daughter, there is no need to bear such a burden because parents always have only love and blessings for their children. You served me for so many years. My love and blessings are always with you.'

Years have passed. My parents, in-laws, and many elderly relatives have passed into Part Two. I have sought forgiveness from each of them and attained completion. I experience immense contentment within due to this. Thanks a lot!"

Kanchan Chandwani

20

Conversing With Non-Living Objects

So far, we have learned about the A-MSY. Now, we will understand the E-MSY in this chapter. Here, "E" means Earth. All the things on earth have an E-MSY. Everything made of soil, wood, steel, or any other metal has an E-MSY. Our house, the furniture at home, clothes, electric and electronic gadgets, vehicles, computers, phones, and books have an E-MSY.

Today, science has also proved that a living essence exists even in inanimate things, just like animate beings. The subtle vibrations in inanimate objects constitute its subtle body or the E-MSY, be it a car or the keys of the car. In the Bhagavad Gita, too, Lord Krishna has said that the same consciousness pervades every particle in the universe. Although the level of consciousness is relatively low in inanimate objects, each object vibrates at a particular frequency. When we communicate with the E-MSY of any object, it has the same effect as it would on the A-MSY of any living being.

We often live in extremes. In one extreme, we get attached to things and fear losing or breaking them. In the other extreme, we bang or throw things in a fit of anger. We are being taught to go beyond these two extremes and love everything without attachment. We should not only invite the E-MSYs of objects to get our work done but also to convey our love and gratitude to them. Going forward, this habit can save us from many problems.

Let us understand how to communicate with an E-MSY in different situations. You can either follow all six steps, or you can skip a step as needed.

On losing something

The secret is that nothing is ever 'lost' in the universe. If you have lost something and if you communicate with its E-MSY, then there is every possibility that you will get the lost thing back unless someone has intentionally taken it away. Let's understand it with an example.

Gaurav had to go to the office early for an important meeting. As he was about to leave his house, he realized his car keys were missing. He searched around every corner of the house but in vain.

Like Gaurav, has it ever happened that you have lost something or forgotten where you kept something important and ended up searching for it in distress? If it has, you can communicate directly with that object's E-MSY.

In this example, Gaurav was upset about not finding his car keys. He can communicate directly with the key's E-MSY in this manner:

1. "Dear divine E-MSY of my car keys, I welcome you into my field of awareness.
2. First, please forgive me for being careless. I have not set up a designated place for you.
3. You have always supported me, but I have never valued you. Please forgive me for this. From here on, I will always keep you in a designated place.

4. Wherever you are, please do come into my sight. Only you can save me from being late for the office.
5. I heartily thank you for your support. Thank you... Thank you... Thank you..."
6. For some time, visualize and feel how it is like to hold the keys in your hand and use them.

For the smooth functioning of things

You may have heard many people name their favorite car, scooter, bike, and other things with nicknames like Peanut, Dolly, Baby, Betsy, Ruby, Pearl, Bon Bon, Furby, Babe, and so on. This shows that they dearly love their belongings and treat them like living beings. In India, people worship their belongings and thank them on the day of the Dussehra festival. Industrialists worship their factories, carpenters worship their tools, and shopkeepers worship their shops and ledgers. When we express gratitude for these things, they support us for several years.

There could be situations where you are cooking food for special guests at home and the grinder suddenly stops working. Or you need to work on some documents on the computer urgently and the computer is not turning on despite trying everything. You want to access information on the Internet but cannot connect.

Such incidents happen every now and then, and our work is stuck. In such a situation, if you know the E-MSY prayer, you can communicate with the gadgets' E-MSY and set them right. Here is an example of communication with a laptop's E-MSY:

1. "My dear laptop's divine E-MSY, I welcome you into my field of awareness.
2. Please support me in my important work today.

3. Please forgive me for not taking care of you properly. From here on, I will take good care of you. For now, please fix yourself and support me. Thank you... Thank you... Thank you..."

Besides a laptop, you can communicate with the E-MSY of your TV, refrigerator, mobile, or any other electronic gadget and seek their support in a similar way. You can also communicate with the E-MSY of intangible objects like the Internet service, or the electric supply to restore the service if it is disrupted.

While traveling

Often, many people are very apprehensive while embarking on a journey. They are afraid of meeting with an accident. They are anxious about their safety all the time. In this case, one can communicate with the vehicle's E-MSY to safely transport him to his destination. The mode of transport can be road, rail, air, water, or any combination of these. Suppose you are traveling by bus. Touch the bus with love and assert:

1. "Dear divine E-MSY of the bus, I welcome you into my field of awareness.
2. Please leave me safely at my destination ---- (name of the place).
3. Take care of your safety and the safety of my co-travelers and me.
4. Thank you so much for making our journey pleasurable, peaceful, and joyful."

While purchasing something

Besides the above, if you wish to buy things like a scooter, car, house, or mobile, communicate with their E-MSYs. If your neighbor buys something, you need not feel jealous that "He has it, and I don't."

Using the power of direct communication, you can communicate with the E-MSY of that thing, "Please come into my life; I am ready to receive you." Then see the miracle! Everything will begin to flow smoothly toward you.

If you ask for something with pure intention and no selfish motive, it reaches you quickly. If you want something unique that is miles away, it will start moving toward you with the E-MSY prayer.

To ensure positive vibes in the house

The house we live in also has an E-MSY. When we worship, offer prayers, and perform other rituals in the house, we actually purify and thank the house's E-MSY. Its walls bestow peace upon us and help us live lovingly with our family. While lovingly touching the walls of the house, we can communicate with its E-MSY:

1. "Dear divine E-MSY of my beloved house, thank you so much for always bringing peace and comfort to me and my family.
2. When I return home after a long, exhausting day, I experience a unique peace. Thank you so much for that.
3. My dear house, may you always brim with love, joy, and peace, and help us dwell in love, joy, and peace.
4. I and my family members may have knowingly or unknowingly polluted your vibes with our disputes, negative thoughts, and feelings. I seek forgiveness for that.
5. Henceforth, I will maintain your sanctity not only externally but will also strive to preserve holiness internally with meditation and prayers."

Gratitude toward the Earth

The earth is like our mother. We dwell in her lap. She nurtures us. She is the very substratum of everything, including the living and non-living beings, on our planet. We are alive because of her, so we must thank her. We must express gratitude toward her and also, seek her forgiveness for having caused all the destruction through deforestation and environmental pollution.

To summarize, we can communicate with everything around us in easy and simple words when needed. When non-living objects are lost or disrupted, we need to increase our tuning with them, which will help fix the problem.

The E-MSY prayer

You can practice the following prayer to express your love toward objects or services for their smooth functioning.

1. "Dear divine E-MSY of … (name of the object or service), I welcome you into my field of awareness.
2. I am grateful to you for your contribution and unconditional support in my life. I thank you from the bottom of my heart.
3. You have completely supported me in attaining success and mental peace.
4. You have always cooperated and supported me, but I never appreciated or thanked you due to my ignorance and insensitivity. Please forgive me for that.
5. Please forgive me for any shortcomings in taking care of you.
6. Please forgive me for not witnessing the Almighty in you and considering you a mere object that is different and inferior to me.

7. I promise that from here on I will value your love and support. I will care for you. I will witness the same consciousness in you as there is in me.
8. Please forgive me for whatever I have done due to my foolishness till today.
9. Thank you… Thank you… Thank you…"

Testimonial - 7

Conversing with Animals' A-MSYs

Besides humans, all living beings dwelling on earth, in water, air, and the sky contribute equally to nature's working. They are all similar in nature, be it human beings, plants, organisms, animals, or birds. They all have A-MSYs and B-MSYs, but for some exceptions. Hence, instead of regarding them as superior or inferior, we should treat them alike. Their level of consciousness alone differs.

God has never discriminated in all that He has created. But due to humans' carelessness, some organisms have been synthesized since many years with only a gross body. They are pathogens like certain bacteria and viruses that multiply in certain unclean or biochemically conducive environments and harm human health. These organisms do not have an A-MSY. However, organisms like insects and other animals that have naturally evolved without human intervention have an A-MSY.

When we see insects breeding in homes, a question arises about how to treat them. To deal with this issue, we can invite their A-MSY into our field of awareness and communicate with them. Although their language may differ, their A-MSY is intelligent enough to understand all languages. Whichever language you use to communicate with it, it will follow what you say.

Let us read about two such experiences in this regard.

> "Despite daily cleaning, we were facing a cockroach menace in our home. I didn't like them freely moving around in the house. I couldn't opt for pest control also because we were taught since childhood, 'Don't kill insects. It is a sin. God's presence exists even within them. Practice non-violence.' Then a prayer arose within me to get rid of the cockroaches with love, not with violence. Maybe, I had encroached on their habitat. So, I sought their forgiveness.
>
> One day, while I was meditating, it suddenly flashed to me that the A-MSY prayer could be practiced here. It was a Eureka moment! Then I invited the A-MSY of the cockroach into my field of awareness and clearly communicated, "My home is extremely clean. Please let me keep it clean. You can move to any other conducive place." I also visualized a border line and requested them, "This is a border line for you. Please do not ever cross it. You are free to live beyond these limits." I practiced this prayer for a fortnight. And you won't believe it! Today there is not a single cockroach in my house!"
>
> *Sandhya Shah*

***

You may have seen farmers erect scarecrows in fields to protect the crop from birds. You can also invite birds' A-MSYs into your field of awareness, communicate with them, and make them understand. Have faith; they will accept your request, as shared in the following experience.

"Now, I have befriended birds very well. There was a time when they would ruin the flowers and litter in my garden. I invited them into my field of awareness, prayed, and lovingly communicated with them, 'Please enjoy the food grains and water kept in the bird bowl. Please help me to keep the garden clean. Let the flowers that are blooming in the flowerpots be as they are. I never pluck them because I love them very much.' Since then, the birds have neither spoiled the garden nor the flowers. Thank you!"

Dr. Chetana

***

Similarly, if you are also facing a problem or are in the dilemma over how to behave with these beings, these experiences will surely help you. In the process, you will develop greater tolerance and deeper compassion as well.

Testimonial - 8

Communicating with Objects

It is often seen that some people not only blame others for their problems but also hold lifeless objects responsible for their problems. For example, one happily shifts to his new house. After that, if some adverse incidents happen in his life, he faces some difficulties, or his family members fall ill, he blames the new house for that, "This house is inauspicious. Ever since we have shifted here, we are constantly facing some issue or the other," and so on.

Similarly, if there is a problem with any electronic appliances like the mixer-grinder, refrigerator, or TV, people immediately start blaming them, "Ever since I have purchased this mixer/TV/refrigerator, my expenses have doubled!"

They don't realize that by talking negatively about these things and blaming them, they are disturbing their tuning with these objects and thus harming themselves. Instead, they could have communicated with the E-MSYs of these objects and gained their support in such adverse circumstances.

Some people have befriended inanimate objects and reaped immense benefits. Have faith that if you communicate and befriend them, they will always be ready to safeguard you and work for you consistently.

Some seekers, who always thank these friends and take care of them, have shared their experiences.

> "I am a professor at Sanjeevani College, Kopargaon. I still remember that day in 2013 when I was riding on my motorbike from Sangamner to Kopargaon. It was around eight in the evening. As I passed Zagade Phata, suddenly, three thieves overtook my bike. One of them snatched my bag. My bike slipped, and I fell onto the other side. As the road was under construction, rocks were heaped by the roadside. Two of the thieves started pelting stones at me. But all the stones hit my helmet, and my head remained safe. One of them tried to escape with my bag on my bike, but the bike wouldn't start.
>
> So in panick, they dropped my bike and ran away on their own vehicle. Surprisingly, all the stones they threw at me hit my helmet, and I still use the same helmet. Usually, I use my helmet only while going to college. I don't use it while going out of town. But that day, my wife insisted, 'Please return home early. You always return late.' I nodded and walked into the parking. While cleaning the bike, I prayed to its E-MSY, 'Dear divine E-MSY of my bike, may my journey be safe and help me return home safely.' As I started the bike, a thought occurred, 'Today, I will use the helmet.' So, I put it on.
>
> As the thieves left, I got up from the shrubs, picked up my bike, and tried to kickstart it. The thieves had tried to kickstart the same vehicle many times but in vain. And here, I tried to kickstart it and it started with a single kick. The

thieves stole the cash, receipt books, and my laptop from my bag. So, I registered an FIR at the police station. It was almost midnight when I reached home. I narrated the whole incident to my wife and sought forgiveness. I heartily thanked the E-MSY of my bike and helmet and calmly went to bed as if nothing had happened.

The next day, when people came to know about this incident, they said, 'You have lost your laptop; you won't get it back.' My Ph.D. thesis was stored on the laptop. I had faith, 'Nothing is lost. Whatever is mine will come to me for sure.' I continued praying to the laptop's E-MSY every day. Within a month, I got my laptop back! I have full faith in the power of the E-MSY prayer that played a significant role in this miracle."

Dr. Subhash Patankar

***

You, too, can communicate with your phone, laptop, or vehicle daily and experience this miracle for yourself. If not daily, you can at least express gratitude to them every time you use them so that they can help you consistently. Sometimes, we misplace things like keys, important papers, or other valuables, and try as we might, we cannot remember where we kept them. In such a scenario too, we can communicate with their E-MSY and request them to come into our sight or give us a hint to locate them. Thus, we can consider these inanimate things as living beings and benefit from them. Let's read the other experience of a seeker.

"After learning to drive a car, I bought a second-hand car excitedly. I would lovingly take care of it and keep it clean. Whenever I would drive over a pothole, I would enquire,

'Are you fine?' I would also heartily seek forgiveness from it. Before every journey, I would pray for its best support and thank it on returning. I would never miss getting its servicing done periodically. I didn't even realize how three years had passed while communicating with the car's E-MSY and using it lovingly with care.

One day, I was driving to Pune with my family (my wife, two-year-old son, younger sister, and mother). My sister and mother, seated in the rear seat, started meditating. My wife and son had put on the safety belt and were seated on the codriver's seat. I was driving the car. It was early morning, and the car raced past the highway. Suddenly the tyre burst, the car wobbled, and came to a grinding halt amongst the roadside shrubs. The car was in a bad shape. Surprisingly, all of us were completely safe and could get out of the car without any harm. I fully believe that all this could happen only because of my tuning with the car. It supported us so caringly. Now, my conviction has grown stronger that the so-called non-living things also understand our feelings!"

Manish Punjabi

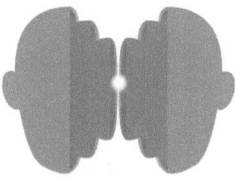

PART 4

Using the Power of the A-MSY for Your Spiritual Awakening

21

Preparing for the Afterlife

Suppose you want to travel to a new country. You need to know the rules followed there before you embark on the journey as every country has different rules and laws as per its governance.

Similarly, some laws of earthly life do not hold good in the afterlife, i.e., in Part Two. We all know that we have to travel to Part Two at some point in time. Then, why not gather its information in advance so that we can start preparing for it from now itself?

One may think, "I will think about it when the time comes. Why should I waste my time now?"

But we do not realize that we will reap the benefits of our preparations right away! We will see its effect in our earthly life itself. Then we may wonder, "Oh, if I had known this earlier, I would have abided by these laws."

Better late than never. Let us start now. We will understand this sense of urgency with the help of a story.

Everyone lived happily in a village. One day, the head of the village gave a shocking news to the villagers, "Now, our time in this village is over. Years ago, a contract had been signed whereby we would live here till a certain date only. After that, we have to move to another village with different rules of living.

Here in this village, you have been living your own way. Society has been divided according to caste and creed. There is discrimination. Some castes are considered superior to others. Social standing, fame, and wealth are held above everything. But in the new village, people donning a particular kind of costume are highly regarded. People wearing clothes made of a particular type of cotton are considered superior and are respected."

The villagers listened eagerly to the head and further enquired, "Sir, please tell us what are the other things considered important there? We want to know more about the other village, so we can start preparing from now on."

As per the headman's guidance, the villagers started preparing for everything that would be useful in the new village. Earlier, if the weight of their clothing was even slightly heavy, they would take it off and throw it away. But now they started practicing wearing heavy garments of fur.

Now all the villagers had only one goal. They began making all the preparations that would help them in the new village. They abolished all the discriminatory titles conferred upon them earlier according to their social standing, wealth, status, and caste. Their attitude of superiority was wiped out.

Earlier, the villagers were into different kinds of businesses. Some ran hotels, some theatres, some earned by selling adulterated food products, while some were into the liquor business. Now, all these businesses were closed. The villagers got a clear direction. They were awaiting the news.

Today, you are also receiving great news. Even after the end of this earthly life, your life will continue! It does not stop here. It will only exist at a different frequency.

We must understand what are those things that we considered very important in Part One but that have no role to play in Part Two.

For example, someone is busy only with earning money or eating food all his life. On reaching Part Two, he realizes that this was a double loss! The first loss was that he spent his entire life amassing wealth and indulging the senses, which has no role in Part Two. And the second loss was that while doing so, he didn't learn anything else. After reaching Part Two, he began to think, "Part One was much better than this!" He does not see any possibility of getting out of Part Two because he doesn't have a physical body that can age or die anymore. He sees no end to his journey in Part Two. His condition is miserable. It's neither fish nor fowl!

But if he is used to seeking guidance in Part One, he can learn a lot in Part Two also. He can receive guidance there as well. If he is a learner, he can still find his way. Otherwise, he will keep complaining, "What the hell is this!"

In Part One, one faces a lot of troubles and sorrows due to the limitations of their B-MSY. Besides this, they have to fulfill many desires like earning money, keeping healthy and stress-free, and working on their tendency of negative thinking. But these limitations of the B-MSY end when one moves into Part Two. The requirement to gather health, wealth, and prosperity no longer remains. The A-MSY is so agile and fast in Part Two that whatever one thinks about manifests instantly!

While transitioning to Part Two, the B-MSY has already been left behind and only the A-MSY exists. Hence, it is necessary to attain the training to use the powers of the A-MSY with the right understanding during one's life on earth. Otherwise, being ignorant of the powers of the A-MSY, one uses them to fulfill their trivial mundane personal desires. It is just like asking Aladdin's genie to pick up a matchstick!

All the comfort and conveniences you earned here will be left behind when the physical body perishes. Only your feelings, thoughts, and pious acts will accompany you in Part Two. So, you can gauge the significance of training your thoughts. The more your mind is aligned with positive thinking and chaste feelings, the more it will support you in your life in Part Two.

Hence, one must plan their life keeping in mind both Part One and Part Two. The realm of Part Two is beyond the dimensions of time and space. It works with the power of thoughts. Your desired object is bestowed upon you as soon as it arises in your mind, like a wish-fulfilling divine tree, regardless of whether it is positive or negative. The moment you aspire for something, it manifests immediately. You don't get the time to think before manifestation. However, time and space play an important role in manifesting thoughts into reality in earth life. When you desire something on earth, you need to rigorously think, rethink, and contemplate it. And it also takes some time for the desire to be fulfilled. In the meanwhile, you can also change your desire. Since there is no such time constraints in Part Two, you need to train yourself right here, on earth, to lend the right direction to your thoughts.

Hence, it is said that life on earth is a short visit and attaining a human birth is the greatest boon. Here, we get the ground for our spiritual practice along with the people around us as our co-creators.

If you keep both your lives in Part One and Part Two in mind and start learning from now on and inculcate new habits accordingly, then your whole life, including Part One and Part Two, will be beautiful. You will have harmonious relationships with everyone on earth and imbibe all the divine qualities. Moreover, you will continue progressing higher in your journey in Part Two.

22

Training the Intuitive Mind

Till now, we have understood that Part One and Part Two together constitute our complete life. We must work on ourselves and train our mind right here in Part One so that our mind can scale new heights in its journey in Part Two.

Part One is actually a training ground for our mind. We take up academic projects where we undergo practical training meant for our career ahead. Similarly, the people and circumstances during our life on earth are tailor-made for training the mind and developing vital qualities required in the life hereafter. If we learn to balance and control our mind in Part One, our A-MSY can easily progress higher during its journey in Part Two. As our life in Part Two is solely driven by our thoughts, working with a controlled mind is essential.

One may question, "How to control the mind which hankers after one desire after another like a monkey?"

To accomplish this herculean task, we must first understand the structure of the mind before we train it. For the purpose of understanding, let us divide the mind into two parts—the intuitive mind and the contrast mind. Let us understand how beautifully the intuitive mind works and how the contrast mind entangles us due to ignorance.

The intuitive mind doesn't indulge in comparisons and judgments. Thoughts naturally arise from within for whatever work has to be done and one is completely engrossed in completing the work. The intuitive mind does not label anything as good or bad. The work has to be completed, it is being worked upon, and it gets completed. This is the intuitive mind. The work done by the intuitive mind is always graceful, worthy of compliments, and creative because there is no resistance.

For example, a small child playing in the soil also eats the soil. If someone scolds him, he cutely laughs at them. His intuitive mind is active. There is nothing good or bad for him. The intuitive mind is focused only in the present without any past or future, labels of good or bad, honor or humiliation, inferiority or superiority, etc. Hence, the more life is driven by the intuitive mind, the more the A-MSY supports us. When a mature person works from this state of mind, everything happens in a free flow. There is amazing power in this state of free flow.

If we want to always work with our intuitive mind, we must get rid of our contrast mind first. The contrast mind is that part of the mind that keeps popping up in the form of countless thoughts during and after the work is completed; it tries to take credit for everything without doing anything; it plants the seeds of doubt. For example, a student is studying with an intuitive mind. His contrast mind keeps disturbing him intermittently, "Stop it. It is so boring. It's been two hours. It is enough for today. Exams are yet to come. You are intelligent. You can manage it. You can do it later," and so on.

The power of the contrast mind is scattered because the contrast mind is fragmented. Therefore, whenever you work with your contrast mind, many things go on simultaneously in your mind, and the outcome is ineffective.

Imagine that you are at a crowded fair. You want to cut that crowd out. Your entire focus is only on the empty space through which you can find your way out. There are some acquaintances and strangers in the crowd. But you have nothing to do with them. You just look for space to get out of the crowd.

This is the state of the intuitive mind. It always focuses on the present task. In the above example, your only goal is to get out of the fair. You don't see anything else. Your intuitive mind is completely focused on this task. In such a situation, some people make space for you while some are adamant and spare no space. But you ignore them. You only connect with those who give you space. Thus, space will be created and you will find your way out smoothly.

The contrast mind will say, "It is impossible to get out of this crowd." This is because it always compares things as "Good" or "Bad." It makes assumptions and weaves its own stories that hinder the smooth working of the intuitive mind. But if the intuitive mind is active, it will guide you safely out of the crowd. Later you will realize that it was indeed impossible to get out of there. In fact, when the intuitive mind works, all the unseen powers also help us go in the right direction. This is the intuitive mind—a hidden warrior, a dark horse.

A dark horse implies that the hidden powers within you manifest when the time comes. Till that moment, you are unaware of them. Then you wonder, "How did I do it!"

For example, when you see a lean and thin person, you think, "He is so weak! What will he do if he has to suddenly defend someone? If he is unable to protect himself, how will he help others?" And suddenly, you encounter a scene where he fights with all the assaulters and drives them away. You wonder, "He has great courage! I never knew it!" This is a hidden warrior.

Similarly, astonishing miracles can happen in your life when your A-MSY is supported by the intuitive mind and discerning intellect!

So, communicate with your A-MSY to eliminate the contrast mind and let your intuitive mind work smoothly. Start watching yourself in situations and ask your A-MSY to alert your intuitive mind as soon as the contrast mind is activated. Whenever the contrast mind compares, tries to reason out logically, takes credit, and somersaults in fantasies, then you must be able to assert, "This is the thought of the contrast mind. I won't give it power. I must ignore it." Gradually, you will observe that the power of your contrast mind will weaken and end. Then, your intuitive mind will remain active all the time. We have come to the Earth school to train ourselves to allow the intuitive mind to work all the time.

As soon as an incident occurs and the contrast mind starts blaming the situations, the people around you, or if negative thoughts start running through your mind, then communicate with your A-MSY immediately and ask for its support. Also, request your mind to work intuitively. Then, your A-MSY will support you fully in that situation.

With the support of your A-MSY, your discerning power will awaken. It will bring many new dimensions of your mind and thoughts to light that will pave the way for your highest development. These new dimensions also help you with your journey in Part Two.

23

Invoking the A-MSY of a Higher Consciousness

India is a holy land, where sages and saints have contributed toward its upliftment for centuries. After long years of penance, they attained Self-realization and gained an understanding of the Truth. They preserved these insights in the form of idols and scriptures. They intended that people should contemplate on the idols and scriptures, decode the profound secrets of the truth hidden in them, understand and assimilate them in their life, and experience pure consciousness that is beyond form, by grasping these decoded messages. These forms were meant to be a bridge toward the experience of the formless consciousness.

All the idols of deities and the holy scriptures from all religions serve as the medium to guide us toward the supreme Truth. These sacred creations are an expression of divine qualities. The higher consciousness dwells within them. And people have deep faith, conviction, and love toward them. You can seek their help by inviting their A-MSYs into your field of awareness. The higher consciousness can also consist of your ideals, universal energies,

Self-realized masters, trustworthy guides, spiritual guides, masters, messengers, and so on.

The divine qualities of the idols you worship or the higher power that you may have faith in automatically start getting suffused within you. Similarly, focusing on the qualities of the ones you adore, your guide, or someone you regard highly also brings a transformation within you. Hence, you can invite their A-MSY into your field of awareness and seek guidance.

When you invoke a divine power and seek something from it, that thing automatically starts gravitating toward you. It may be a worldly desire, a unique quality, or a higher prayer. Let's understand this through a story.

One day, Maharshi Valmiki was seated on the banks of the Tamasa River. He noticed a beautiful pair of crane birds calling to each other and mating. He felt happy seeing the happy birds. Suddenly a hunter's arrow pierced through the male bird and killed it instantly. The shocked female bird began to moan loudly. Maharshi Valmiki was so much moved by her pain that his heart flooded with compassion, and spontaneously, a healing hymn arose within him. He was surprised on listening to the hymn. He returned to his hermitage wondering, "How did this hymn arise?"

Lord Brahma appeared before him then and explained, "I inspired this hymn to arise within you. Moreover, many more such hymns will come to you, and a beautiful epic will soon emerge from within you! You must start penning them down."

With inspiration from Lord Brahma, Maharshi Valmiki sat down to write. But he experienced an emptiness within. Not a single hymn arose! He was worried as to what he should do. He invited Sage Narada and asked, "Please tell me, why is no hymn arising within me?" Sage Narada advised him, "Please invoke Goddess Saraswati, the Goddess of Knowledge. When you pray to Her from the bottom of your heart, she will surely help you." Soon, with the blessings of Mother Saraswati, hymns gushed within Maharshi Valmiki like a stream, and a beautiful epic was composed. That epic later came to be known as the Ramayana.

This story explains the significance of divine power. It depicts how invocation connects you with higher consciousness and how that consciousness begins to express itself through you.

When you invoke such a glorious power into your field of awareness, what will you ask for? Of course, you will ask for supreme qualities! It is like, when you visit a diamond shop, you will not ask for a mere precious stone! You will ask only for the solitaire. Similarly, when you come face to face with your deity, your guru, or your mentor, what will you seek from them? You will surely ask for the diamonds of devotion, faith, wisdom, surrender, understanding, love, bliss, and supreme peace so that you are liberated forever from entanglement in the game of joy and sorrow; you can attain the goal for which you have come to earth.

Prayers also arise according to one's level of consciousness. If one wants love, he will pray for love. If one wants to be immersed in devotion, he will pray for devotion. One will yearn for guidance if he is lost in the mists of confusion. And only if one yearns for supreme liberation will he pray for the ability to grasp and assimilate the understanding of the truth. The more one's level of consciousness elevates, the higher the prayer.

We should strive to develop the cognizance of the divine power and pray for supreme qualities. But how do we pray to the divine? Let us understand this and then practice it.

Invoking the A-MSY a Higher Consciousness

1. Invite the A-MSY of your revered one into your field of awareness. "Dear divine A-MSY of my Supreme Lord/my Guru/Universal Energy/guide, I invite you into my field of awareness. I welcome you."

2. Pray heartily, "Dear Lord/Idol/Guru/Universe, please fill my life with love, joy, and peace. Please bless me with the power of your devotion. May my life be smooth, simple, and beautiful. Please liberate me from every futility and fill me with divine devotion."

3. Now seek forgiveness, "You have showered me with immense love and bliss, yet I race behind illusory pleasures. Please forgive me for being entangled in this."

4. Assert with conviction, "I have complete faith that you have the power to eliminate my ego and tendencies and awaken divine devotion within me. You are capable of liberating me from my confusion. Hence, please start working on it."

5. Chant calmly within, "Love, Joy, Peace... Love, Joy, Peace... Love, Joy, Peace."

    Now, with utmost love and respect, request the A-MSY of your revered one, "You may now leave my field of awareness and continue to support me ceaselessly. Please be there with me forever."

6. Express your gratitude, "Thank you... Thank you... Thank you..."

In this way, invoke the A-MSY of a divine power into your field of awareness with a feeling of devotion. Let yourself blossom entirely. Witness the wonderful expression of this higher consciousness all through the journey of your life.

24

Seeking Your A-MSY's Support for Spiritual Progress

In ancient times, saints and sages (spiritual scientists) would practice penance amid the discomforts of the Himalayas to work on their spiritual quest. At times, they would be immersed in meditation for years together without any food and water. You may wonder, "How could they meditate for so long, free of worries, far away from their homes, amid fierce wild animals, and in the wrath of harsh weather? How could they go on without any guarantee of food, covering long distances in the quest for water, having no assured place to rest, and no connection with their family and relatives? How could they bear the endless climatic challenges with intense rains, scorching heat, and chilling winters? How could they make it possible?"

You may say that they were already bestowed with spiritual powers, or they had strong willpower, or their B-MSYs were healthier and stronger. But the fact is that they took full support of their A-MSYs for penance. They were very well aware of the powers of the A-MSY. They used these powers to the best of their ability to attain their spiritual goals. With time, this wisdom has been lost to the world and very few are aware of it today.

Now, we are understanding the applications of this wisdom in contemporary language. The lost knowledge is being brought to light again. For every person who considers inner growth as their final goal, this knowledge is no less than a key to the ultimate treasure.

Situations have changed with time. People's mindsets and ways of living are also different now. The world is full of illusions. If a common man wishes to renounce these illusions, his family and responsibilities toward them pull him back. The biggest limitation is his own body which is not ready to support him. Illnesses of the body and their treatment impose restrictions on him. But this doesn't mean that he should leave his spiritual journey or give up his inner progress, because his ultimate purpose in life is to work on his inner growth and realize the Self. Hence, today, you are advised not to be an ascetic but to be a balanced human, and balance your life beyond the polarities of materialism and asceticism. A-MSY communication and the tools of meditation and prayer are given to you for your inner growth.

This is a powerful tool for inner spiritual practice that can help you guide your tendencies, desires, and sensory cravings in the right direction, wherein the powers of your A-MSY will help you scale new heights in life.

It is a great challenge to live in self-conscious awareness while carrying out worldly responsibilities among people with different behavioral patterns. The A-MSY prayer can help immensely in carrying out your spiritual practice in such situations. When a seeker practices meditation, his contrast mind often leads him astray. Sometimes, a discomfort in the body, such as numbness of limbs or the sensation of insects crawling, sleepiness, restlessness, or paying attention to the outside noises distract him during meditation. Then the seeker loses his focus or meditates for a very short time. You can communicate with your A-MSY before meditation and request it to help you go deeper in meditation, retain the focus, and also seek the support of your B-MSY.

If you aim to attain the pinnacle of inner growth, you will strive to raise your level of consciousness with awareness. You will refrain from things that lower your consciousness. Before meditation, invite your A-MSY into your field of awareness and request it to liberate you from your tendencies and habits that pose obstacles in attaining your goal. Communicate with it to help you improve your concentration.

In ancient times, seekers would tie their hair to something to avoid falling asleep during meditation. Whenever they would fall asleep, their hair would get pulled, and they would snap out of slumber. But you don't have to do this today because you are now aware of the secret of A-MSY communication that can save you from such obstacles in meditation.

To maintain concentration and remain receptive during meditation, first communicate with your A-MSY as follows and then meditate:

"My dear divine A-MSY! Please be calm, stable, and relaxed. Please help the B-MSY remain healthy and undisturbed despite any physical pains, hot or cold sensations, or problems due to weather changes while I meditate. You can do this. You can also seek support from the A-MSY of that part of the body that is experiencing trouble or pain. Be present with complete surrender. Please support the Self in experiencing Itself. You are helping the Self by remaining healthy. You have the power to make all this happen. Please start working on it. Love, joy, and peace have the power to make this happen. They can keep the body healthy and stress-free, help it align with nature, and balance the flow of energy. Hence, please support them. Love,

Seeking Your A-MSY's Support for Spiritual Progress

Joy, Peace… Love, Joy, Peace… Love, Joy, Peace…Thank you… Thank you… Thank you…"

To attain your ultimate goal in life, you can communicate with your A-MSY in the following way and seek its support before you meditate:

1. "My dear divine A-MSY, I welcome you into my field of awareness.

2. I have great respect for you. Please awaken divine qualities in me so that I can attain the supreme goal of my life. May my life brim with love, joy, and peace. May my feelings, thoughts, speech, and actions be aligned and integrated. May my life be prosperous physically, mentally, socially, financially, and spiritually.

3. Please forgive me for using my qualities only for illusory and material gains to date. Henceforth, I will use all my qualities, keeping my highest goal in mind.

4. Thank you so much for making this happen."

5. Close your eyes and chant for a while. Chant the name of your deity or guide, and then say, "My dear divine A-MSY, please return to your place. Please continue to support me even after leaving my field of awareness.

6. Thank you for supporting me in my spiritual quest and helping me with your powers to attain my ultimate goal. Thank you… Thank you… Thank you…"

Testimonial - 9

Benefits of the A-MSY in Meditation

When it comes to meditation, many complain that they cannot sit in one place for a long time, or they can't sit down for meditation, or sometimes their mind is lost in thoughts, so they can't meditate.

In such a situation, you can inform your A-MSY before meditating, "This is my time for meditation. Pain, sensations, and discomfort are only in the gross body. So, please take care of them. Even if thoughts arise, tell them, 'This time is dedicated for meditation alone. We can deal with the thoughts later. There is a whole day ahead for thinking on all other things.'" Then your A-MSY will handle all these issues and support you to dwell in an unwavering meditative state. Let us read two experiences related to this.

> "I could easily meditate for a short time. But whenever I would meditate for long, whether seated on a chair or cross-legged on the floor, my B-MSY would soon stop supporting me. I would experience pain in my legs and unknowingly straighten them. This would break my meditation. Then, if I tried to continue, I would feel numb in my legs, sitting

in the same position. Else, there would be some itching as if something is biting me. Obviously, it would be difficult for me to meditate, and my eyes would open. I didn't understand why this was happening. Then I heard about the art of A-MSY communication and started communicating with my A-MSY before meditation, 'I am going to meditate now. Please take care of the sensations that arise in my body during the meditation. Please handle all the pains and discomforts that hinder my meditation. Let the impact of the weather changes, be it cold or hot, not disturb me. Please ensure that my thoughts don't distract me. Let me be fully receptive, united with the higher consciousness. Please bless me. Thank you so much.' Thus, I started meditating after communicating with my A-MSY. And now, my B-MSY fully supports me to meditate for a long time."

Nitin Masurkar

***

"I meditate at a fixed time every morning. I wished to extend the duration of meditation. Also, considering my supreme goal of life, I felt the need to meditate at any time during the day. But I could not attain this. This made me feel restless. Then I prayed to my A-MSY to support me in increasing the duration of meditation and it has made it possible! Now, I meditate two to three times a day. Moreover, I am able to meditate with great ease at any time."

Sandhya

Likewise, if you also seek the support of your A-MSY to attain your supreme goal, it will surely help you in every possible way.

25

How To Attain Balance in All Spheres of Life

Q1: How can we know if our A-MSY communication has brought the desired outcome?

You can request your A-MSY to give you indications that your prayer is being answered. Those who consistently communicate with their A-MSYs witness changes in their lives; all their troubles end. But in the beginning, it seems difficult to understand the outcome of A-MSY communication.

Suppose you asked for help from your A-MSY for a project. Then you can request your A-MSY for an indication, "My dear divine A-MSY, I am relentlessly working on a project and giving it my best. Please indicate that the project is going to beget the best results."

We often pray for the health of our family and friends. At that time, we can pray, "My dear divine A-MSY, please give me a hint that the health of my relative or friend has begun to improve." You will start receiving signals in different ways, which will deepen your faith that the work has started. Many a time, we interrupt our prayer by worrying. Even in that case, asking for an indication will end that interruption.

Besides this, the biggest block gets created in one's life when one starts thinking negatively after the prayer. To avoid this, he should pray, "Please give me a hint that my prayer is being answered." Have faith that you will start receiving signals not only for this prayer but for all the prayers you have offered for which you wanted indications. You just have to be aware and alert to recognize the indications. Let's understand this with an example.

A person had gone for a picnic and suddenly remembered that the cupboard back home was probably left open. He was anxious throughout the picnic thinking, "I left the cupboard open. What will happen now? Will there be a theft? How forgetful I am! I always commit some blunder. What do I do now?" Since he couldn't do anything, he called upon his A-MSY and prayed, "The cupboard is left open at home. Please take care of it and give me some hint that you are doing so." Suddenly, he heard a carpenter telling his assistant, "I have locked the door." Although he was talking in a different context, this person was alert as he had asked for indications. He was surprised, "Oh! This indication was for me!" It is evident from this example that when you ask for indications, they will be delivered to you in every possible way.

Sometimes the indications will be very clear and you will catch them instantly. But sometimes, you may be confused, "Is it true or not? Is it definitely for me? I don't even know. Should I believe it or not?" In such a situation, you can pray, "Please give me clearer hints and the understanding to recognize and decode them. If the indication is to do something, give me the courage to act upon it. I lack clarity about what I should do and should not, or how it will happen. Please give me clear understanding for that." In this way, you can pray to your A-MSY for clear indications, courage, and faith.

Q2: When we communicate with the A-MSY, how does it function? I am unable to logically understand how the A-MSY communication brings about a change within.

Suppose a child wants to draw on paper. He will first make an outline on the sheet of paper with a pencil and then color it with crayons or darken it with sketch pens. If the outline is drawn correctly, the drawing will have the right shape. But if the outline itself is distorted, the drawing would also be distorted. The same applies to our gross and subtle bodies. Just like the outline drawn by a pencil is close to the paper, the subtle body is close to the supreme consciousness. If the subtle body is powerful and healthy, it will affect the gross body accordingly.

The paper represents the Universal consciousness that pervades everything. Since the A-MSY is very close to the consciousness, as soon as you communicate with it and seek its support, it connects directly with the supreme consciousness. Then, the supreme consciousness and the A-MSY work together, due to which we receive favorable results.

Now, if you want to make some changes to the drawing, you can easily erase the pencil outline and draw a new outline. But the same is not usually possible if the outline is drawn with a sketch pen. You will have to work harder to change it. The outline drawn with a sketch pen represents the gross body. Thus, it is easier to work on the subtle than the gross level.

For example, you want to wake up a child. If the child is lazy, you will have to call him out several times. Similarly, if you wish to make some changes in your gross body, you will have to repeat the process multiple times. But if you wish to make changes in the subtle body, you won't have to do that; it brings faster results. As we have understood, only thoughts work in Part Two. So, it is easy to create anything with the A-MSY using our thoughts. Earlier, since we didn't know this, we tried making changes in our gross body with the help of our subconscious mind, which took a long time. But now, changes can happen immediately by directly communicating with our A-MSY.

For example, if you want to get your work done by someone, and he is not a close friend, you try to reach him through a common acquaintance. If that person also does not know him well, he will ask someone else. So, when there are 4-5 people involved in the process, it takes time to get the work done because they all are connected indirectly. You keep reminding them, and they keep telling you, "Yes, I will do it. I will meet that person tomorrow. I will remind him." Amid all this, your work gets delayed. But if you directly contact the person who is doing your work, your work gets completed quickly. In the same way, when we communicate directly with our A-MSY, transformation begins immediately within us.

The onset of any disease or tendency first happens in the subtle body. Later, it manifests in the gross body. Then we start treating it. Hence, if we work at the subtle level, the disorder will end there itself, and its manifestation on the gross body will not happen at all.

Q3: Can we request the A-MSY to develop new skills like writing or communication?

Yes! You can communicate with your A-MSY to receive training from the A-MSYs of experts in any field, "I want to develop this skill within me. Please guide me in doing so."

Most of us know the story of Guru Dronacharya and Eklavya in the Indian epic, Mahabharata. Eklavya revered Dronacharya as his Guru, created his sculpture, and practiced archery before it. In fact, Eklavya invoked Dronacharya, i.e., he welcomed Guru

Dronacharya's A-MSY into his field of awareness and sought guidance from him. Even today, some people pray to Goddess Saraswati (the Hindu Goddess of knowledge, music, art, speech, wisdom, and learning) to bestow upon them skills in writing, music, and the ability of discernment. Some also practice their skills in front of the Goddess's idol. Others pray to Lord Hanuman for strength and fearlessness. People invite their A-MSYs and request them to bestow their qualities or talents upon them. Nowadays, almost everyone prays to Goddess Lakshmi for wealth, opulence, and prosperity. So, this means you need to invite and communicate with the A-MSYs of gods, goddesses, or the experts whose qualities you want to imbibe. You can also request your A-MSY to seek those qualities from them.

Q4: How can students communicate with their A-MSYs for knowledge and expertise in a subject they want to graduate and excel in?

Suppose you are pursuing electronic engineering and want to seek complete knowledge about the subject. You can communicate with your A-MSY, "I invite the A-MSYs of all the experts, masters, and pioneers of this field into my field of awareness. I wish they impart their knowledge to me. I am fully receptive. I also invite love, joy, and peace into my field of awareness so that I receive everything with love. May all the experts in the world guide me. Let them give me as much as I can receive." Besides communicating with your A-MSY, gain knowledge from all the people, books, and articles you come in contact with, related to your field. Have faith that you have to attain mastery in this field as per your divine plan. Communicate to nature that you are in favor of mastery. You will soon find that all the required information is flowing toward you or you will be guided to places where this information is available.

Q5: Can we practice group communication with the A-MSYs of multiple people?

Of course! If you want to share something with your entire family or group of friends, you can invite their A-MSYs into your field of awareness.

Imagine you are out of station and wish to connect with your family. You create a video conference link and invite everyone on the call. The names of all those you intend to call are added to that group. Likewise, you can invite everybody's A-MSYs with their names and communicate with them. You can share what you want with everyone simultaneously.

Such a group prayer is practiced at Tej Gyan Foundation three times a day, i.e., at 6:15 am, 3:30 pm, and 9:00 pm (IST), for world peace and healing. You, too, can participate in it and reap its benefits.

Q6: What should we visualize when we invite our A-MSY into our field of awareness? What is the A-MSY like?

Whenever you invite your A-MSY into your field of awareness, be peacefully present. Be aware without any imagination. Some feel that they see a light while some see a picture, depending on their nature. Everyone's nature is different. Whether you see something or not, you just need to train your mind to remain calm, without wandering here and there and support you in your A-MSY communication, giving the A-MSY a chance to work by itself.

Q7: When we are inclined more toward spirituality or more focused on stabilization and meditation, it doesn't seem easy to focus on other fields. So, what should we do to balance all spheres of life?

Everything is easy if practiced in the right way and with discipline. There is no dearth of time, but we feel so due to a lack of discipline and we believe that while completing one task, we have to leave other tasks incomplete. This is not true. It is just a game of the mind. If the mind is disciplined, it knows it has to stay calm when it is time for meditation, study, or work. Otherwise, whenever you begin a task, the mind keeps reminding you of all the other tasks that are pending. To avoid this, first train your mind to be disciplined. Instruct your mind, "I have reserved the next two hours for study," or work, or whatever you intend to do. It could be exercising, meditating, reading a book, etc. And if it still interrupts, remind it, "The rest of the day is available for doing other things. Let me focus on the current task right now." When you train your mind this way, it learns to remain disciplined and starts supporting you. You only need to train your mind consistently.

Suppose you have determined to exercise your body for good health, do it regularly. If your mind is not ready to work on it for long, focus for the bare minimum time that you can work on it. Then dedicate the decided time to it fully. Be completely receptive even while studying. Your consciousness and A-MSY will also support you in doing so. Everything will be disciplined with patience and time management. Your Self-stabilization, studies, knowledge, all work in the physical world, and prayers, together with discipline, patience, and training your mind, will bring the results you desire. Everything will support one another.

Q8: What is the difference between the Self and the A-MSY? Who communicates with the A-MSY from within us?

The Self is the source that is common for everyone. The A-MSY has immense, unlimited power that runs the B-MSY but is invisible to the human eye. The A-MSY and B-MSY of each person are separate. The Self is universal. It is the consciousness that pervades everything due to which our body works. The A-MSY and B-MSY work as long as they are connected to the Self. But the **Self has always been... is... and will be there forever...** The play of the subtle and gross body continues in the presence of the Self.

Just as when several words are written in different colors on a paper, the colors and words are different, but the paper in the background is common! This background paper is akin to the Self, the Universal Being.

The Self plays the role of an individual and invites the A-MSY into its field of awareness. The Self runs the A-MSY and B-MSY... the one who drives the scooter... in whose presence everything happens... it is the "Real You."

Appendix 1

Testimonials

A complete life which is lived with a holistic understanding of both Part One and Part Two can be attained by mastering the A-MSY. It is rightly said, "Do only one task at a time with diligence, and all the other tasks will be completed automatically." For example, if you water the roots of a tree properly, all the leaves, branches, flowers, and fruits flourish on their own.

You often experience that if you attain one thing, everything else is attained automatically. For example, if you learn a language, you can easily understand all the books, audios, and videos in that language. Similarly, if you master communication skills, you attain harmony in relationships at the office, at home, and among friends. Thus, after attaining certain things, all other things related to them are automatically attained.

Many seekers who gained this knowledge are witnessing the glory of A-MSY communication. While thousands have witnessed such miracles, the experiences of only a few of them are shared here due to the limit of pages in the book.

"Happy Thoughts! I am Dr. Ananta Gore, from the town of Khamgaon, Maharashtra, India. I am a gynecologist. I have witnessed miraculous results in my profession with the A-MSY prayer. I wish to share one of those experiences with you.

A lady was in her third trimester. Her blood pressure had gone above 210/120. She fell unconscious due to complications, and the baby died in her womb. Her hemoglobin count was around four to five and her condition was very critical. I called her family and informed them, 'Her condition is very serious. We couldn't save the baby and her life is at risk.'

With the consent of her family, the patient was taken to the operation theatre. We arranged for four to five bottles of blood and started the surgery. As we started, the patient suddenly stopped breathing. She passed into Part Two. I was shocked! I was stunned as to how this had happened. I then prayed to her A-MSY, 'You can't leave like this. You have to return.' The situation was very critical for a minute. Emergency medication was given to the patient. Suddenly, she resumed breathing and started talking to us. This was nothing less than a miracle!

Then the patient was shifted to the I.C.U. But there was a new problem. Her urine output was zero. She had a kidney injury. I invited her A-MSY into my field of awareness and communicated, 'You can heal yourself. You have divine power. Please heal your gross body.' I invited her kidney's A-MSY into my field of awareness and communicated with it in the same manner. This way, I communicated with all her affected organs one by one and requested them to heal themselves. This went on continuously.

Then the patient was shifted from Akola to Mumbai's J.J. Hospital. I continued to pray to her A-MSY every morning, noon, and night. A month later, her husband came to meet me and said, 'Now my wife is completely fine and healthy. There are no issues. After dialysis for two to three days, everything is back to normal. The urine is also passing smoothly. Kidneys, too, are normal. Everything is fine now.'"

Dr. Ananta Gore

***

"I am Mrs. Dhanashree Chougule. I tested positive for Covid on 9th August 2020 and was admitted to the hospital. I could easily accept the situation as per the understanding received from Tejguru Sirshree and I started practicing the A-MSY prayer.

Three days later, I was diagnosed with an advanced stage of pneumonia. I was shifted to the I.C.U. The oxygen level dropped so much that I was finding it difficult to breathe. But still, my mind could remain stable. The situation worsened suddenly at night. Then, I invited the A-MSY of my lungs into my field of awareness and communicated with them. It was a confluence of medications, blessings, and assertions. And soon, I learned that a special, hi-tech ventilator had been arranged for me. Soon my breathing came back to normal. I continued the A-MSY prayer throughout the night. Everything was back to normal by morning. My oxygen levels had also increased. The A-MSY prayer is truly magical."

Smt. Dhanashree Chougule

***

"I am Suhani Sharma from Mumbai. I got married two years ago. A few months after marriage, I was diagnosed with tuberculosis of the lungs. Doctors opined that the disease is drug-resistant, so I would have to be administered high-potency drugs. Within six months, the disease was cured, but due to the side effects of the drugs my hearing ability was impaired and I became deaf.

The sequence of these incidents led me into depression. Then a yoga teacher introduced me to a doctor from Tej Gyan Foundation. The doctor taught me the unique method of A-MSY communication. I also practiced forgiveness. My husband and I sincerely practiced it for 21 days every morning for half an hour. This helped me come out of depression and I started becoming happy. Then I sought treatment for three months which helped me regain my hearing ability. The A-MSY prayer is very simple, but we must practice it regularly. I am obliged to the Tej Gyan Foundation family."

Suhani Sharma

***

"I am a retired government officer from Pune. I have been associated with Tej Gyan Foundation since 2003. One of my close relatives tested positive for Covid. He was admitted in the Covid ward of a hospital for ten to twelve days. His condition was deteriorating. I used to call him daily and give him all the mental support possible. It brought him some relief.

When he returned from the hospital, he called and told me he was fine. But one day, suddenly, he called and said, 'I feel mentally stressed. Anything can happen to me at the moment. My body is also shivering with fear.'

I immediately remembered the A-MSY prayer and assured him, 'Don't be afraid. Sit quietly with your eyes closed for ten minutes. Open your eyes only when I call you.'

I then prayed to his A-MSY with complete faith. Then I called him and asked him to open his eyes. Within half an hour, he called me back and asked with wonder, 'What magic did you perform that I am now feeling completely healthy and peaceful? All my fears ended suddenly. The noise of my thoughts has also calmed down. Now I am feeling much better.'"

Dhananjay Kulkarni

***

"One day, I lost my precious gold ring. All my family members began looking for it. We searched through the entire wardrobe but didn't find it. I thought, 'How can I be so careless? It's a big loss.'

Then, I remembered the E-MSY prayer explained by Sirshree. I invited my ring's E-MSY into my field of awareness and said, 'Wherever you are, please come into my sight. You are very precious to me. I didn't take care of you properly, so please forgive me for this.'

As I finished praying, a voice said from within, 'The ring is in the wardrobe.' As my faith grew, I was convinced that I would find my ring in the wardrobe only. And one day, I suddenly found the ring hidden between some clothes. I am firmly convinced that if we pray from the bottom of our heart, it will only bring positive results. We just have to be patient."

Sunita Therokar

***

"I am Manisha. I have been practicing the A-MSY prayer since I heard about it from Sirshree. I prayed for the positive changes I wished to see in my daughter and husband. I wanted my daughter to be fearless, so I invited her A-MSY into my field of awareness and asserted, 'You are fearless. You are courageous.' By praying this way every night, I found my daughter becoming courageous day by day.

Similarly, I prayed daily to bring positivity in my husband's thinking and found amazing results. Now he thinks very positively. His perspective has changed.

I practice this prayer with many people like doctors, shopkeepers, auto-rikshaw drivers, etc. I wish you, too, practice the A-MSY prayer with complete faith and take full advantage of it."

Manisha Dustakar

Appendix 2

A Survey Report Highlighting the Importance of Prayer and Meditation

According to a survey based on a CNN (Cable News Network) poll, 73% of adults believe that praying for others also heals them, and 50% of patients want their physicians to pray along with them.

This survey shows what people want. People believe that prayer will help them feel happier and more contented. They will experience satisfaction after a medical appointment accompanied by prayer.

A fresh survey, "Survey 1", published by the National Institute of Health, found the ten most common treatment techniques practiced in America. Three of them included prayer, wherein 43% of the participants prayed for themselves and 24% for others by participating in prayer groups and offering individual prayers.

Jeff Levin, Professor of Epidemiology and Population Health at Baylor University, has stated that there is a correlation between religious and spiritual participation and health. More than 1600 experiments have been conducted in this regard. The findings from these studies were astounding. These findings are consistent irrespective of the religion people belonged to, their ailments or health conditions, age, gender, race, caste, or nationality. These results are positively associated with education. People with a strong academic background believe that the practices of meditation and prayer are important for their complete health and well-being.

Today, 101 medical schools have included syllabi on spirituality for patient care in their programs. In 1995, the number of schools that included a spiritual syllabus was 17, which is now rising. The UCLA Medical Center and other such hospitals encourage physicians to include patients' spiritual history in their medical charts.

This makes it clear that rituals like prayer are becoming a part of mainstream medicine. Dr. Harold G. Koenig, working at Duke University, suggests that doctors should ask every patient whether they consider themselves spiritual or religious. If the response is positive, the doctors should promote prayers and religious participation for them. He believes that prayer has the power to heal and it is our responsibility to give importance to that power along with medication. In spirituality, hope and the power of positive thinking are directly related.

In 1955, Henry K. Beecher proved that between 16- 60% of patients — 35% on average— benefited from placebos for healing pains, coughs, mood swings from medication, headaches, sea-sickness, and the common cold. They were told that the only cure for their condition was a placebo. Now, placebos are only used for testing in clinics, and 35% people respond to it, on an average. It has been concluded from the study of the placebo effect that our faith is so powerful that it can influence our health outcomes.

Meditating for 10 to 20 minutes twice a day slows down the metabolism, heart rate, breathing, and brain activity. It also helps cure chronic pains, insomnia, anxiety, feelings of hostility, and depression. Besides this, it has been found to be beneficial for infertility and premenstrual syndrome (physical, mental, emotional, and behavioral symptoms experienced by a woman before menstruation). Moreover, it is highly supportive in treating cancers and HIV.

Dr. Herbert Benson calls the process of meditation as "relaxation response." He concluded, "The more serious a disease becomes due to stress, the more the relaxation response needs to be activated. This is an extremely effective treatment for it."

It has been observed in various studies that 60- 90% of the patients suffer mostly due to stress. The process of relaxation and meditation is taught to them. It is proven to be effective for patients with chronic pain, hypertension, headache, and irritable bowel syndrome.

This research data clearly shows the effectiveness of prayer and meditation in treating various ailments. The powerful healing technique of A-MSY communication works like a wish-fulfilling tree at the subtlest plane of creation. So, you can gain whatever you wish, gross and subtle, tangible and intangible, in all the facets of life. Like the sages and saints of yore, you can use it for attaining the ultimate purpose of life i.e., Self-realization.

* * *

You can mail your opinion or feedback on this book to:
books.feedback@tejgyan.org

About Sirshree

Sirshree's spiritual quest, which began during his childhood, led him on a journey through various schools of philosophy and meditation practices. He studied a wide range of literature on mind science and spirituality. After a long period of deep contemplation on the truth of life, his quest culminated in attaining the ultimate truth.

Sirshree espouses, "All spiritual paths that lead to the truth begin differently but culminate at the same point – Understanding. This understanding is complete in itself. Listening to this understanding is enough to attain the Truth." Over the last two decades, he has dedicated his life to raise mass consciousness.

Sirshree has delivered more than 4000 discourses that throw light on this understanding. He has designed a system for wisdom, which makes it accessible to all. This system has inspired people from all walks of life to progress on their journey of the Truth. Thousands of seekers join in a virtual prayer for World Peace and Global Healing daily at 9:09 am and 9:09 pm.

About Tej Gyan Foundation

Tej Gyan Foundation is a non-profit organization founded on the teachings of Sirshree. The Foundation disseminates Tejgyan – the wisdom that guides one from self-development to Self-realization, leading towards Self-stabilization.

The Foundation's system for imparting wisdom has been assessed by international quality auditors and accredited with the ISO 9001:2015 certification. This wisdom has been presented in a simple, systematic, and practically applicable form that makes it accessible to people from all walks of life, regardless of religion, caste, social strata, country, or belief system.

The Foundation has centers in more than 400 cities and towns across India and other countries. The mission of Tej Gyan Foundation is to create a highly evolved society by leading seekers from negative thoughts to positive thoughts and further, from positive thoughts to Happy thoughts. A 'Happy thought' is the auspicious thought of being free from all thoughts, leading to the state of supreme bliss beyond thoughts.

If you seek such wisdom that leads you beyond mere knowledge, dissolves all problems, frees you from all limiting beliefs, reveals the true nature of divinity, and establishes you in the ultimate truth, then it is time to discover Tejgyan; it is time to rise above the mundane knowledge of words and experience Tejgyan!

The MahaAasmani Magic of Awakening Retreat

Self-development to Self-realization towards Self-stabilization

Do you wish to experience unconditional happiness that is not dependent on any reason? Happiness that is permanent and only increases with time? Do you wish to experience love, peace, self-belief, harmony in relationships, prosperity, and true contentment? Do you wish to progress in all facets of your life, viz. physical, mental, social, financial, and spiritual?

If you seek answers to these questions and are thirsty for the ultimate truth, then you are welcome to participate in the MahaAasmani Magic of Awakening retreat organized by Tej Gyan Foundation. This is the Foundation's flagship retreat based on the teachings of Sirshree.

The purpose of this retreat

The purpose of this retreat is that every human being should:

- Discover the answer to "Who am I" and "Why am I?" through direct experience and be established in ultimate bliss.
- Learn the art of living in the present, free from the burden of the past and the anxiety of the future.
- Acquire practical tools to help quieten the chattering mind and dissolve problems.
- Discover missing links in the practices of Meditation (*Dhyana*), Action (*Karma*), Wisdom (*Gyana*), and Devotion (*Bhakti*).

About Books by Sirshree

Sirshree's published work includes more than 150 book titles, some of which have been translated into more than 10 languages. His literature provides a profound reading on various topics of practical living and unravels the missing links in karma, wisdom, devotion, meditation, and consciousness.

His books have been published by leading publishing houses like Penguin, Hay House, Bloomsbury, Wisdom Tree, Jaico, etc. "The Source" book series, authored by Sirshree, has sold over 10 million copies. Various luminaries and celebrities like His Holiness the Dalai Lama, publishers Mr. Reid Tracy, Ms. Tami Simon and Yoga Master Dr. B. K. S. Iyengar have released Sirshree's books and lauded his work.

The Source
Attain Both, Inner Peace and Worldly success

Awaken the Power of Faith
Discover the 7 Principles of the Highest Power of the Universe

To order books authored by Sirshree, login to:

www.gethappythoughts.org

For further details, call: +91 9011013210

Tej Gyan Foundation – Contact details

Registered Office:
Happy Thoughts Building, Vikrant Complex, Near Tapovan Mandir, Pimpri, Pune 411017, INDIA. Contact: +91 20-27411240, +91 20-27412576

MaNaN Ashram:
Survey No. 43, Sanas Nagar, Nandoshi Gaon, Kirkatwadi Phata, Off Sinhagad Road, Taluka Haveli, Pune district - 411024, INDIA. Contact: +91 992100 8060.

WORLD PEACE PRAYER

Divine Light of Love, Bliss, and Peace is Showering;

The Golden Light of Higher Consciousness is Rising;

All negativity on Earth is Dissolving;

Everyone is in Peace and Blissfully Shining;

O God, Gratitude for Everything!

Members of Tej Gyan Foundation have been offering this impersonal mass prayer for many years. Those who are happy can offer this prayer. Those feeling low or suffering from illness can receive healing with this prayer.

If you are feeling troubled or sick, please sit to receive the healing effect of this prayer. Visualize that the divine white healing light is being showered on earth through the prayers of thousands and is also reaching you, bringing you peace and good health. You can dwell in this feeling for some time and then offer your gratitude to those offering the prayer.

A Humble Appeal

More than a million peace lovers are praying for World Peace and Global Healing every morning and evening at 9:09. This prayer is also webcast on YouTube at 9:00 pm. Please participate in this noble endeavor.

www.ingramcontent.com/pod-product-compliance
Lightning Source LLC
LaVergne TN
LVHW041712070526
838199LV00045B/1308